Para–Platforms

Para–Platforms
On the Spatial Politics of Right-Wing Populism

Markus Miessen & Zoë Ritts (eds.)

Sternberg Press

7 Introduction
Markus Miessen & Zoë Ritts

12 Sketch for a Theory of Design Politics
Mahmoud Keshavarz

25 The Leaderless Digital Counterrevolution
Angela Nagle

41 So Heavy Grasshoppers: Allochthonous Notes on Populism
Benjamin H. Bratton

53 In the Name of God
Slavs & Tatars

Para–Platforms: Symposium, November 2017

59 *Introduction*
Markus Miessen

61 *The Case of Trump & Brexit*
Hannes Grassegger

83 *Rechte Räume*
Stephan Trüby

107 *The NSU Case*
Christina Varvia

133 Template Culture: Parameters of Political Design Themes for the Internet
Konrad Renner

139 Imagining Terror: Propaganda Art Today
Jonas Staal

155 Negative Internationalism and Shame as Strategy
Nina Power

160 Solidarity without Sameness
Patricia Reed

166 Interview with Wolfgang Tillmans

178 Let's Talk about Fascism
Hito Steyerl

186 The Stone
Markus Miessen & Zoë Ritts

189 To Fit Reality to Their Lies, 2018
Liam Gillick

197 Biographies

201 Image Credits

Introduction
Markus Miessen & Zoë Ritts

Right-wing populism is not new. Yet our current historical conjuncture presents emergent and extreme forms that demand critical inquiry. This is true at the level of the spatially imagined, the virtually performed, the designed and physically built—as each in different ways is facilitating the unprecedented development of ring-wing political energies. In Europe, neo-Nazism, fundamentalism, and hate-based ideologies rooted in violent patriarchies have gained institutional acceptance and political sponsorship at a variety of scales. Populist and authoritarian tides are sweeping through the West, in France, Italy, Hungary, and across the Atlantic.

This project investigates new movements through space, methods for enacting extremist politics such as the invasions into our most private digital worlds. This project also investigates new patterns of occupying space, such as the nebulous post-public online communities of the far right, or even the gradual appropriation of entire European villages by neo-Nazi groups emerging here and elsewhere.

Three case studies of emergent spaces of right-wing populism, presented in a symposium organized by Markus Miessen at the Gothenburg Design Festival in November 2017, form the core from which this collection of essays has grown. These investigations were presented by Stephan Trüby, Hannes Grassegger, and Christina Varvia of Forensic Architecture. Each of the three contributors presented tactics which question how design, whether interpreted as research or as the adaptation of existing tools, can play an active role in responding to (spatial) politics. Stephan Trüby's presentation emerged from his project on Rechte Räume, a long-term research project on the habitation and occupation patterns of neo-Nazi groups in Europe, which is currently ongoing in coordination with Markus Miessen.

In the opening lines of his essay in this collection, Mahmoud Keshavarz reminds us that design "is the very practice that constitutes conditions for certain politics to happen."[1] The interrelationship between design and politics is implicit. Given this foundational tenet, our contributors were prompted to go beyond critique, toward identifying ways in which designers, artists, thinkers, and spatial practitioners can rectify political violence in our (designed) environments. By presenting a broad collection of voices, this volume, intended as an introduction to a range of methods and approaches, aims to generate a prismatic vantage onto the designed spaces of right-wing populist politics in Europe, abroad, and online.

Concurrent with the reemergence of extremist political trends, a wealth of recent discourse has sought to reflect on the tensions and tactical weaknesses of the fungible form that is "populism." Populism can be manifested in a variety of political valences, so it is necessary to declare a specific focus on right-wing populism in the pages that follow. Here, the recent scholarship by Corey Robin is useful: "Conservatism is about power besieged and power protected. It is an activist doctrine for an activist time. It waxes in response to movements from below and wanes in response to their disappearance."[2] The emergent right-wing populism in Europe is, as others have commented, a threat-based response united by anti-immigration, anti-liberal, anti-elitist, and anti-progressive sentiments, easily combined with other specific, particular conservative opinions and taken to violent extremes.

As has also been widely discussed, recent major shifts in European politics have resulted in a situation in which even the most stable social-democratic parliaments have been subject to successful populist tactics implemented from the extreme right end of the political spectrum. In Sweden, the Sverigedemokraterna (Swedish Democrats) are currently on the rise—without even mentioning the worrisome examples of Austria, Italy, France, the Netherlands, Hungary, or Poland, to name only a few. In Germany, the Alternative für Deutschland (AfD) has been injecting a *völkisch*-authoritarian populism that mobilizes a racist vocabulary in order to access precarious voter demographics. This strategy is most successful in areas which are exposed to structural deficits not only in terms of institutions and economies, but in regard to a weakened civil society that might collectively claim space. This has resulted in a diversity of carefully designed parallel platforms, established in order to both physically and virtually assist the development and rise of nationalist and populist struggles. These political struggles go hand in hand with projects of accumulating and appropriating spaces, whether symbolically, virtually, or in hectares.

There is nevertheless significant variety and differentiation within useful definitions of populism. Scale offers one useful rubric for sorting out these expressions. Operating at the scale of the individual subject, right-wing populism clearly emerges from the psychological devastations of neoliberal social policy and structural economic instability. Lacking traditional means of social support, disenfranchised individuals now routinely turn to communities founded on hateful and violent views. These groups clearly position themselves as benefactors of a declining welfare state. At the scale of the nation, new identitarian nationalisms have taken root around the collapse of traditional borders and walls, again linked to economic globalization. In this context, the violent dialectic Wendy Brown terms "walled states/waning sovereignty"[3] has given rise to new populisms founded on the violent rejection of refugees, immigrants, and a host of related scapegoats. Finally, while planetary urbanism has created important possibilities for cosmopolitan citizenship, it also results in new scales of right-wing populism. One can look to online worlds where "discontiguous megastructures"[4] of digital-communication and existence result in social atomization and dislocation. Thus, we encounter the emergence of loose, transnational social networks united by misogyny, racism, or other myth-making projects based on spurious supra-nationalism and others.

Many of the contributions in this volume take a speculative tone for possible alternatives. This project does not attempt to comprehensively document the spaces of right-wing populism, though such a project is both worthy and needed, but aims rather to present an array of research and tactics. It understands the nature of right-wing populist politics as inextricable from the spatial formations facilitating those politics, and presents designers and thinkers who respond spatially, materially, and artistically — and with equal force. As Slovenian artist Marjetica Potrč notes: "We are not liberated from space. Even in an age when we inhabit digital space and speak in abstractions about private and public space, we are nevertheless dependent on physical space. As sociologists have pointed out, any group that strives for recognition requires physical space. Placemaking is the creation of such a space. This is where social reality is constructed — in a place."[5]

It is from this particular spatial focus that contributors in this reader outline territory from which we can work toward new social realities that resist the malignant politics of right-wing populism. It is crucial to be attentive to the ways in which these political maneuvers are constructed as social frameworks, substitutions for state infrastructures, spatial or architectural constructs, or in virtual networks. It is these designed structures which—in addition to the hateful rhetoric of their protagonists—need to be addressed.

As Chantal Mouffe argues in her recent book *For a Left Populism*, to intervene in the hegemonic crisis "it is necessary to establish a political frontier and that left populism, understood as a discursive strategy of construction of the political frontier between 'the people' and 'the oligarchy,' constitutes, in the present conjuncture, the type of politics needed to recover and deepen democracy."[6]

In a time in which the popular perception of the contemporary condition has succumbed to a fragile construct devoid of any emotional or affective attachment, in which there does not seem to be a narrative that can overcome the dilemma of resignation and generalizing critique of capitalism, we need to invent new strategies to decrypt and undo the tactics of right-wing populism. *The Design Politics* framework at the HDK Academy of Design in Gothenburg attempts to inhabit this territory: to understand the complexities of identified political situations and to develop design strategies in order to counter them.

1
Mahmoud Keshavarz, "Sketch for a Theory of Design Politics," 12, in this volume.

2
Corey Robin, *The Reactionary Mind* (Oxford: Oxford University Press, 2011), 26.

3
Wendy Brown, *Walled States, Waning Sovereignty* (Cambridge, MA: MIT Press, 2010).

4
Benjamin H. Bratton, *The New Normal* (Moscow: Strelka Press, 2017).

5
Marjetica Potrč, "Self-Organization in Communities Where the State has Withdrawn," in *The Neighbourhood as Global Arena / Reader* (Holon: Israeli Center for Digital Art, 2015).

6
Chantal Mouffe, *For a Left Populism* (London: Verso, 2018), 5.

Sketch for a Theory of Design Politics
Mahmoud Keshavarz

I

This essay is an attempt to formulate an understanding of design as a set of material articulations and modes of acting that manipulate the materiality of the world. Such an understanding recognizes that design is not an external nor an instrumental feature but the very practice that constitutes conditions for certain politics to happen.

To understand the internal relations of design and politics, one needs to frame how design and politics are understood. This essay understands design as both a noun (the designed thing) and a verb (the act of designing), and investigates how both generate practices beyond a single "thing." This design and designing runs the gamut from the articulation of artifacts and artefactual relations to environments, situations and policies, from interfaces to regimes of practices and performances. In this sense, design is understood as an articulatory practice that configures different material artifacts, each with their own technical and artificial components as well as the relations between various artifacts, sites, and spaces that operate within specific social, environmental, and economic conditions.

Politics is here understood beyond a form of police-politics, beyond the one that is concerned with maintaining the order and the status quo. A politics that polices the state of situation is not necessarily exclusive. It rather includes, and at the same time suppresses, possibilities of acting otherwise through recognition of only certain names, identities and defined places and spaces assigned to various individuals, groups, parts, and communities. Politics is here rather understood as the act of distancing oneself from such distributions and formations by requalifying the space and time of political practices by those who are rendered unqualified for doing politics.[1] This happens through a certain undoing, while it opens and creates its own space and time as well. The unqualified appear in "wrong" places and "wrong" time; by doing so, they reveal the hegemonic practices that try to keep such parts meaningful only through one name, one identity. Counter-hegemonic practices like these re-qualify the situation through certain acts of rearticulation of relations among parts by distancing from the state of situation. This reading of politics will, as we shall see, open up toward possibilities of thinking design and politics together as design politics.

In fact, the main argument here is that design cannot but be involved in questions of politics and that understanding "design as politics"[2] and politics as design (not merely "and") requires that design begins to take its involvement in these questions seriously. My overall aim is to shift the focus from design and politics as two separate practices, disciplines, or realms of knowledge to the articulations that the nexus of design politics produces, performs, and generates.

II   Material Articulations

If we propose to understand the designed thing and the act of designing as a series of articulations then new openings in regards to design and its relations to politics arise. Articulation in this context does not refer to speaking well or clearly. Instead, it examines how heterogeneous forces interact and combine to produce effects that are not necessarily identical to the elements existing in the articulation of a force, a thing or an event. "An articulation is thus the form of the connection that can make a unity of two different elements, under certain conditions. It is a linkage which is not necessary, determined, absolute and essential for all time."[3] While articulation is often being considered as a matter of discourse,[4] in practice it is always already materially and historically embedded in the processes of social and political formations. These embeddednesses can be called "tendential combinations" according to Stuart Hall, which are "not prescribed in the fully deterministic sense" but are nevertheless "'preferred' combinations sedimented and solidified by real historical development over time."[5] Thus, articulation is about situating linkages, the ability to connect and recognize disconnections, as well as the possibilities for forging new relations.

Articulations can be understood as a set of negotiations that designers practice in the ways that they manipulate materials and the environment in order to achieve their aims. However, such negotiations cannot always be intentional, and the environment and history from, in, or through which the matter is formed can kick back in and promote some drives more favorably than others. Designers redesign over and over again, they rearticulate the form they have given to matter over a period of time, but they often forget that the form that they impose on materials and the environment is only one of the forms produced and persuaded out of their imposition. Other forms often go unnoticed, are ignored or not taken seriously because they are not seen as designed.

Once a chair is designed, it might be considered to be an artifact providing a particular service to its users and consumers. However, it is always more than that. The designed chair has already performed some sort of designation because it has manipulated the environment by the resources it has used, the skills that were used, the labor that was invested in it, and so on. And because of this, the designed chair cannot exist only in interaction with its intended environment or end-users. Moreover, a chair and the shape of it "is not the shape of the skeleton, the shape of body weight, nor even the shape of pain-perceived, but the shape of perceived-pain-wished-gone. The chair is therefore the materialized structure of a perception. It is sentient awareness materialized into a freestanding design."[6] This points out that the politics embedded in the chair are not enacted merely in the office, living room, or kitchen by its use and function. Rather, the chair is spatially and temporally embedded and oriented in the politics of before, during and after design. This means that it is almost impossible to think of the space and time of design in the limited sense of the place and the time of use. The capabilities of wood, skills, and labor in the workshop as a site of production, and the possibilities of the designed chair being oriented in one direction and not the other thus shape spaces that some bodies can occupy while others cannot. Design is not merely an outcome of environments, but is also a source in the production of environments. Sometimes one is stronger than the other, but this mutual relation is always in place.

Design is thus a practice of articulating materialities of the world which produce certain conditions for inhabiting, accessing, or negotiating with the world. To insist on the materialities of articulations is to acknowledge the artifice of things. The artifice of things affirms that things, for the simple reason that they are made, can also be unmade and remade accordingly. In fact, however, and far more importantly, it states that change is the only possible condition for artifice. The materiality of articulation affirms the possibility of change, reformation, redesigning, reassembling, reconfiguring and remaking and redoing in one way or another. These possibilities of making and unmaking thus mean that the act of articulation is a matter of decision, orientation, direction, and negotiation in design actions. Samer Akkach points this out by drawing on the Arabic word for design:

> [T]asmım (design) … [in] current usage, however, seems to be based on tasmım as "determining," "making up one's mind" and "resolve" to follow up a matter. Thus in linguistic terms "design" is an act of determination, of sorting out possibilities, and of projecting a choice. It has little to do with problem-solving, the prevailing paradigm, as the designer (musammım) seems to encounter choices, not problems, and to engage in judging merits, not solving problems. It is closer to "decision-maker."[7]

The modern use of the term tasmım in the Arabic speaking world reveals the directionality that design actions must always take. This is quite the opposite of western-oriented education on design, where design is often construed as a set of skills, techniques and qualities to solve a problem, a seemingly innocent term, which refers to making things better in general. To think of designed things and design actions as material articulations tells us that design should be considered as a decision and direction embodied in all made things that humans bring into being. Design is conditioned by its orientations, directions and capacities, while at the same time conditioning human beings, things and the world.[8] The designed and designing of articulation of material conditions make various forms of being possible while disarticulating other possibilities. These articulations offer certain orientations and inhabitations while restricting others.

While this internal relation of design and politics seems imperative, the design discourse has not taken seriously the question of politics in design, and if it does, it is often done instrumentally. One reason could be the lack of reflection on two separate, and at the same time overlapping, uses of the term design: The designed thing, and design actions and activities. The latter can be understood both as the act and activity of designing as well as the actions and activities flowing from the designed thing. They are used and discussed interchangeably without much reflection on their differences, on what they do, what capacities they have, and how they move from one environment to another. Confusing the designed thing, the design activity, and processes as well as the activities flowing from that designed thing and the act of designing, makes it hard to distinguish between various ideas of politics and their relations to design, to recognize the articulations that already operate at a specific situation and to form possible rearticulation through designing. Consequently, politics and design are left with only two types of relationship: either design in the service of party-politics and police-politics, or design that carries explicitly political content.

Design in itself, in Herbert Simon's words, is always about "courses of action aimed at changing existing situations into preferred ones,"[9] and I add that this is the case no matter what ideology, content or orientation it takes. While there is a point in this affirmative and dominant definition of design that designers should see the world as something that can be changed, one should always ask: toward whose preferred situations should this call for change happen, and who has the agency to make such calls, to identify the matters of existing situations, and imagine preferred situations through designing? This ontological condition of design, that things are always subject to change in one direction or another is determined by the positions of those who have the agency to rearticulate and reconfigure the materiality of the world. Consequently, this points to an understanding and reading of design as matters of im/possibilities; as matters of politics which arise not as transcendental and metaphysical discursive fields, but as very earthly sites of material negotiations and struggles.

III   A Machine from *the Penal Colony*

An example from Franz Kafka's *In the Penal Colony* may help us to understand further the relations between design and politics. While written in words, one can sense the designerly mind of Kafka through his precise description of mechanic operation. The story starts when a visitor to a penal colony is invited to observe an execution which is to be performed using a device specifically designed to torture those who disobey the rules of the colony. The victim is a soldier who failed to follow an order from his officer. The officer is responsible for the machine, and he is also the one who explains and presents to the visitor how the machine works in a very precise manner. His manner of presentation is similar to the way inventors or designers present their works to their clients and customers. The device consists of three main parts: the bed, the inscriber, and the harrow, which are placed below, above, and in the middle, respectively. The harrow is composed of a series of needles, which engrave the sentence on the back of the convict's body. However, the convict does not know about the sentence, but must learn it within her or his flesh. When the visitor refuses to speak in favor of the machine, the officer, the presenter-cum-executioner, frees the soldier and takes his place in the machine with the words "Be Just!" to be inscribed on his body. However, he dies in horrific pain due to machine malfunctioning. The design of this apparatus and the way it is narrated in the story is extremely elaborated and almost fetishized by the officer, as he believes the machine brings the mystical experience of justice to the body of the condemned. For instance, the officer explains why glass has been chosen to make the harrow:

> [T]o make it possible for everyone to observe the sentence as it is being carried out, the Harrow is made of glass. This caused some technical difficulties in fixing the needles into it, but after a number of attempts it worked. There were no lengths we didn't go to. And now everybody can watch through the glass how the inscription is carried out on the body.[10]

In another part, the officer explains the reason behind the two sets of needles used in the harrow:

> "[T]wo kinds of needle in various arrangements. Each long needle has a short one next to it. The long one is for writing, and the short one sprays water to wash away the blood and keep the inscription clear at all times. The mingled blood and water is then piped into these little channels here and finally into this main channel, and its drainage-pipe leads into the ditch." With his finger the officer pointed out precisely the path the blood and water had to take.[11]

Here, one should understand Kafka's harrow as being beyond the spectacle of torture. Kafka's harrow uncovers the detailed practices of law and their effects on human bodies through a highly designed artefact. How law and rule can be materialized in such a precise and pragmatic way reveals the non-transcendentality of law. Thus, the artifice of design and its power of articulation allows the law to represent itself as absent from such a device, and separate itself from the artificial world. As Katja Diefenbach writes, "the law unhinges its force of law, and transfers it to administrative measures that do not have the status of law."[12]

In a sense, we can look at the harrow as what Michel Foucault calls "dispositif"[13] and what Giorgio Agamben calls "apparatus,"[14] that is, an organization of practices, devices, and meanings that are materially constructed and materially affecting. Kafka's harrow and the detailed and developed design of it, which occupies a major part of the story in the form of presentation, takes us into an interrogative sphere where one can understand

and unpack the transformation of rules into norms and their penetration into bodies in a very material sense and in sensible matters. The main part of the story is the gradual disclosure of how the machine functions, what kinds of materials are used, and how the machine is supposed to bring justice. At the same time, there is no part describing the crime, law, or norm of the penal colony to be followed and respected. From there, we have the inscribed bodies, shaped and formed as a result of the design's imposition on them. Design here is a possible violent agent for the material act of inscription, but also an informing one that provides us with the possibility of disarticulating the practices of law. There are these details and materialities that are enacted as witness to the law in particular, and socio-political structures in general. As a consequence of design's overlap with politics, we are now left with new bodies that are constantly affected and defined by such materialized articulations, or as Léopold Lambert puts it in a reverse formulation, this transforms "each architecture into penal colony machines" because they "somehow inscribe something of the norm in the bodies' flesh."[15] While this story might be considered fictional, the articulations generated by design politics produce real effects in real life. One example follows.

IV   A Bear as a Border Guard

In 2011, the Migration Board of Sweden (Migrationsverket) commissioned the producers of *Bamse*—a popular Swedish children's comic book—to make a special issue on migration. Bamse, already a very well-known national cartoon character famous for advocating values such as equality,[16] was commissioned to play the role of a migration board officer in order to communicate a very strong message to the children of asylum seekers about their status in the future. Bamse's role was to explain that those who do not deserve to stay would be sent back "home," but would still be missed as 'our' friends. In one scene, Bamse tells a stressed and desperate asylum-seeking child that despite being the strongest bear in the world (this famous slogan or capacity of Bamse's is also used as the subheading of the series), he is unable to solve all problems. Such a rationalization of the children's world when it comes to permission for residency is also obvious in the illustration techniques used. Throughout the whole book, nothing is real except the migration board's logo and some direct pedagogic asylum policies. The characters, who are animals, the cars, and the airplane that are used for the planned deportation are all cartoons. The relatives of the deported family welcome the deportees beside the airplane, even though this is not possible in the real world. The use of Bamse and the penetration of laws and rules that are materially effective into the imaginative world of children show the banality that the administration of such hostilities implies. The *Bamse* special comic strip on deportation tries to say that there is nothing wrong with deportation. At one point, one of the characters advises the stressed asylum-seeking child that it should go out and play with its friends if it is stressed. The stress of deportation is just a part of the process as it is staged via the illustration. The technical rationality made through communication techniques and illustrations are nothing new.[17] However, the Swedish Migration Board has been unique in using this technique to convey and persuade children of migrants that deportation is nothing more than a normal part of their lives.[18]

    This rationalization by apparently non-violent means is the other side of the militarization of borders that adopt military technologies, armed forces and private security companies to stop asylum seekers and refugees from moving and migrating. This particular way of militarizing the life of a migrant is also what the *Counterinsurgency Field Manual of the American Army*[19] promotes in its wars against insurgents in countries like Afghanistan and Iraq. This new way of militarization which becomes possible through the manipulative power of design as material articulation is clear in the rhetoric used in the field manual: "Design is not a function to be accomplished, but rather a living process. It should reflect ongoing learning and adaptation and the growing appreciation counterinsurgents share for the environment and all actors within it, especially the insurgents, populace, and Host-Nation government."[20] These lines of argument, which are very similar to Tim Brown's[21] ideas on design thinking, tell us how design has the potential power to make divisions, help establish sets of values and reproduce them in new practices of warfare. The counter-insurgency field manual devotes one chapter to design in which it argues that design "may very well be the most important aspect of countering an insurgency."[22] In the manual's chapter on design, a concept entitled "campaign design" proposes the use of design thinking and practice to promote a process based on mutual learning between commanders, soldiers and representatives of a host nation or, more accurately, of occupied lands. Design, according to the American Army, has great potential if used "properly" and "critically" in new practices of warfare to assure leaders that their soldiers and marines "are ready to be greeted with either a handshake or a hand grenade while taking on missions."[23]

This is not a mere co-optation of design by violent forces, as that would be to take away the manipulative power that design has, and would blame only those who co-opt the concepts for their own sake. Design must face its internal relation to politics and strong manipulative capacity granted by its power over material articulations. Because of such an ontological condition that design has, design is already political even before engaging in any explicitly political issue. Design is already political no matter what it does or how it acts; it produces conditions of politics, of manipulation of lives of individuals and communities, of species and ecologies.

V   Possibilities

Designed things do not come into existence through isolated acts. Technologies, practices, and rationalities merge into each other through the act of designing. The act of designing articulates them into a new articulation seen and understood as a product, a site, a service, or a system. These ways and processes are presented and accepted in certain moments as principal components of modernity, capitalism, colonialism, and (neo)liberalism. Thus, they come to be seen as a "natural" and self-evident bounded whole—a whole which is designed, produced, and consumed in the name of reason and rationality, and as an indispensable part of the status quo.

There is no formula for understanding design politics, nor are there conditions for making it. There are only moments, situations, devices, and things that can lead us to disarticulate and rearticulate possible ways of inhabiting the world. While such possibilities might offer a rearticulation of politics, they also derive from certain politics. Therefore, as much as there are possibilities of politics through design as material articulation and a mode of acting in the world, there is a politics of possibilities as well. Politics of possibilities can be defined here in line with Sara Ahmed who argues, "What we 'do do' affects what we 'can do.' This is not to argue that 'doing' simply restricts capacities. In contrast, what we 'do do' opens up and expands some capacities, although an 'expansion' in certain directions might in turn restrict what we can do in others."[24] Possibilities, therefore, are not simply a set of doing and acting that is actualized, nor are possibilities a set of "not-doing." They are rather certain spatial and temporal orientations that favor some capacities prior to others according to their locality and history. Thus, the question of what capacities to go for and to be potential about, is what should be at stake for those working their ways into and through design politics.

    Design is engaged in making, dividing, and patterning how lives are organized according to certain directions or power positions. The task of those who recognize design as a political agent is to show this internal capacity, and at the same time intervene in certain directions, orientations, and power positions—other than those taken so far or those towards which we are heading. This can be understood as a form of design that is capable of thinking.

This essay is a revised and shortened version of "Chapter 3: Design and Politics: Articulations and Relations," in "Design-Politics: An Inquiry into Passports, Camps and Borders" (PhD diss., Malmö University, 2016).

1
My reading of politics is inspired by Jacques Rancière's notion of politics as a matter of equality and more particularly as acts of "re-distribution of the sensible." See "Design-Politics: An Inquiry into Passports, Camps and Borders," 81–84.

2
Tony Fry, *Design as Politics* (Oxford: Berg, 2010), vii.

3
Lawrence Grossberg and Stuart Hall, "On Postmodernism and Articulation: An Interview with Stuart Hall," in *Stuart Hall: Critical Dialogues in Cultural Studies*, ed. David Morely and Kuan-Hsing Chen (London: Routledge, 1996 [1986]), 131–150.

4
This is mostly notable in the work of Ernesto Laclau and Chantal Mouffe and their use of the term in their book *Hegemony and Socialist Strategy*. For them discourse is the only articulatory practice that constitutes and organises social relations. Thus, specific social formations can be determined by particular discursive practices. In their theorization, articulation happens through discursive points which "partially fix meaning" and allow specific formations of the social to take shape. Ernesto Laclau and Chantal Mouffe, *Hegemony and Socialist Strategy: Towards a Radical Democratic Politics* (London: Verso, 2001 [1985]), 111–113.

5
Stuart Hall, "Race, Articulation, and Societies Structured in Dominance," in *Sociological Theories: Race and colonialism* (Paris: UNESCO, 1980), 305–345.

6
Elaine Scarry, *The Body in Pain: The Making and Unmaking of the World* (Oxford: Oxford University Press, 1985), 290.

7
Samer Akkach, "Design and the Question of Eurocentricity," *Design Philosophy Papers* 1, issue 6 (2003), 324.

8
This is often referred to as an ontological understanding of design. See Anne-Marie Willis, "Ontological Designing," *Design Philosophy Papers* 4, issue 2 (2006): 69–92.

9
Herbert Alexander Simon, *The Sciences of the Artificial* (Cambridge, MA: MIT Press, 1969).

10
Franz Kafka, "In the Penal Colony," in *Metamorphosis and Other Stories* (London: Penguin, 2007 [1919]), 81.

11
Kafka, 81.

12
Katja Diefenbach, "To Bring About the Real State of Exception: The Power of Exception in Agamben, the Power of Potentiality in Negri," *Translate eipcp*, January 25, 2008, http://translate.eipcp.net/strands/02/diefenbach-strands01en#redir. 2008.

13
Michel Foucault, *Power/Knowledge: Selected Interviews and Other Writings, 1972–1977*, ed. Colin Gordon (Ithaca, NY: Random House, 1980), 194–196.

14
Giorgio Agamben, *What Is an Apparatus? and Other Essays*, trans. David Kishik and Stefan Pedatella (Stanford, CA: Stanford University Press, 2009).

15
Léopold Lambert, *The Funambulist Pamphlets, Volume 07: Cruel Designs* (Goleta, CA: Punctum Books, 2013), 46.

16
As a child who was born in the aftermath of the anti-imperialist and anti-capitalist 1979 Iranian Revolution, I started my day by watching *Bamse* broadcast from Iranian state TV each morning. He remained a hero throughout my childhood in his role as the strongest bear in the world who always stood on the side of the poor.

17
The Australian Army has published a comic book targeting specifically (potential) Afghan migrants to deter them from coming to Australia. Their message is clear and written on the first page of the leaflet: "If you come to Australia by boat and without a visa you will not be staying in Australia and be detained on other islands." Furthermore, in West Java, a comic book, *Zero Tolerance for Trafficking in Persons*, is distributed as part of an information campaign to prevent and detect human trafficking. Another comic, *Chimen Lakay*, is distributed in Haiti to reduce irregular migration to the United States.

18
Currently the Migration Board of Sweden had stopped printing and distributing this children's comic.

19
Insurgency is an unconventional form of warfare, which is defined by the US Department of Defense as "organized use of subversion and violence by a group or movement that seeks to overthrow or force change of a governing authority," Joint Chiefs of Staff, "Department of Defense Dictionary of Military and Associated Terms," Joint Publication 1-02, 2010–March 2012, 161. David Kilcullen defines insurgency as "a popular movement that seeks to overthrow the status quo through subversion, political activity, insurrection, armed conflict and terrorism." David Kilcullen, *Counterinsurgency* (Oxford: Oxford University Press, 2010), 184. In response, counterinsurgency (COIN) is a counter-movement to insurgency and is defined as "military, paramilitary, political, economic, psychological, and civic actions taken by a government to defeat insurgency." David Howell Petraeus and James F. Amos, *Counterinsurgency Field Manual: Boulder* (Colorado: Paladin Press, 2006), 2.

20
Petraeus and Amos, *Counterinsurgency Field Manual*, 1–4.

21
Tim Brown, *Change by Design: How Design Thinking Transforms Organizations and Inspires Innovation* (New York: Harper Business), 2009.

22
Petraeus and Amos, *Counterinsurgency Field Manual*, 4–9.

23
Petraeus and Amos, foreword.

24
Sara Ahmed, "Orientations Matter," in *New Materialisms: Ontology, Agency and Politics*, ed. Diana Coole and Samantha Frost (Durham, NC: Duke University Press, 2010), 252.

The Leaderless Digital Counterrevolution

Angela Nagle

It is worth thinking back now to the early 2010s, when cyberutopianism had its biggest resurgence since the '90s, before the dot-com bubble burst. This time it emerged in response to a series of political events around the world from the Arab Spring to the Occupy movement to new politicized hacker movements. Anonymous, Wikileaks, and public-square mass protests in Spain and across the Middle East were getting huge coverage in the news, causing a flurry of opinion and analysis pieces about their profound significance. All of these events were being attributed to the rise of social media and characterized as a new leaderless form of digital revolution. The hyperbole and hubris of the moment should have been enough to make anyone skeptical, but most on the left were swept up in the excitement as images of vast crowds in public squares appeared on social media and then in the mainstream media.

Books, social media, and countless gushing columns and blogs celebrated the arrival of what cyberutopians of the early Internet had long prophesized. To pick one typical example of the tone at the time, in Heather Brooke's paean *The Revolution Will Be Digitized: Dispatches from the Information War*, she claimed, "Technology is breaking down traditional social barriers of status, class, power, wealth and geography, replacing them with an ethos of collaboration and transparency." *Adbusters*, the Canadian anti-consumerist magazine, published a widely shared article by Manuel Castells called "The Disgust Becomes a Network" when leaderless encampments, organized online, started to appear in Spain and around the world. He argued that what he had been writing about for most of his career—the networked society—had taken a radical new form. BBC journalist Paul Mason wrote *Why It's Kicking Off*

Everywhere, documenting the revolutionaries in Tahrir Square, the Iranian "Twitter revolution" and the heavily hashtagged Occupy Wall Street protests that spread around the world.

But this fervor died down in just a few short years. The Egyptian revolution led to something worse—the rule of the Muslim Brotherhood. Islamists ran riot in the streets and stories of rapes in the very public square that had shortly before held so much hope came to light. Soon the military dictatorship swept back into power. The Occupy Wall Street demonstrators remained literally aimless and were eventually forced out of public property by police, camp by camp. By the end of 2013, a public-square-style movement took place in Ukraine, which started with many of the same scenes of romanticized people-power in the public square. However this time the leaderless network narrative, which was already starting to look a little less convincing, was left aside because the protests quickly erupted into fascist mob rule.

In many of the events that *were* considered part of the leaderless digital revolution narrative, like Occupy Wall Street and the public-square protests in Spain, in which thousands occupied the Puerta del Sol, the Guy Fawkes mask was adopted as a central symbol. But the online origins of the mask and the politically fungible sensibilities that can be traced back through the mask should have offered a clue that another very different variety of leaderless online movement had potential to brew.

After the election of Trump, everyone wanted to know about a new online right-wing movement whose memetic aesthetics seemed to have infiltrated sites from the popular The Donald subreddit to mainstream Internet culture. In the lead-up to the election, the most famous common imagery was of Pepe the Frog. The name given by the press to this mix of rightist online phenomena including everything from Milo to 4chan to neo-Nazi sites was the "alt-right." In its strictest definition though, as an army of Internet pedants quickly pointed out, the alt-right term was used in its own online circles to include only a new wave of overtly white segregationist and white nationalist movements and subcultures, typified by spokespeople like Richard Spencer, who has called for a US white ethno-state and a pan-national white empire modeled on some approximation of the Roman Empire.

The movement's media also includes Scottish video blogger Millennial Woes, Red Ice, sites like Radix, and the longform and book publishers Counter Currents.

In the broader orbit of the alt-right, made up of often warring and sectarian factions, there is an older generation of white advocates who pre-date the alt-right but who the alt-right reads and draws influence from, like Jared Taylor from the site American Renaissance who refers to himself as a "race realist" and figures like Kevin B. MacDonald, editor of *Occidental Observer*, described by the Anti-Defamation League as a primary voice of anti-Semitism for far-right intellectuals. The alt-right is, to varying degrees, preoccupied with IQ, European demographic, and civilizational decline, cultural decadence, cultural Marxism, anti-egalitarianism, and Islamification but most importantly, as the name suggests, with creating an alternative to the right-wing conservative establishment, who they dismiss as "cuckservatives" for their soft Christian passivity and for metaphorically cuckholding their womenfolk/nation/race to the non-white foreign invader.

Then there is a range of more obscure rightist anti-egalitarian reactionary tendencies like the earlier neoreaction movement or NRx, which includes thinkers and bloggers like Mencius Moldbug and Nick Land, creators of the influential ideas of "the Cathedral," and the latter, the "Dark Enlightenment." The idea of the Cathedral closely resembles Marxian critical theory's understanding of ideology, as an all-encompassing system and prison of the mind. The Dark Enlightenment is an ironic play on the idea of the Enlightenment, based on a suspicion of progress and rejecting the liberal paradigm. Among all alt-right thinkers Land is the greatest misfit, once closer to the radical accelerationist school of thought and still a highly idiosyncratic thinker, he is not so easily categorized. Within the radical right libertarian pro-tech tendency, common preoccupations include Bitcoin, Seasteading—Peter Thiel's idea to create a separate state off the coast of the US—and rightist elite applications of transhumanism.

But of course what we call the alt-right today could never have had any connection to the mainstream and to a new generation of young people if it only came in the form of lengthy treatises on obscure blogs. It was the image-and humor-based culture of the irreverent meme factory of 4chan and later 8chan that gave the alt-right its youthful energy, with its transgression and hacker tactics. The Guy Fawkes mask used in the protests in 2011 was a reference to Anonymous, which took its name, leaderless anti-celebrity ethic, and networked style from the chaotic anonymous style of 4chan. *V for Vendetta*, which the Guy Fawkes mask is taken from, and the "dark age of comic books" influenced the aesthetic sensibilities of this broad online culture.

While commentators praised the rejection of the right-left divide among a new wave of Internet-centric protest in the early 2010s, the political rootlessness of this networked, leaderless, Internet-centric politics now seems a little less worthy of uncritical celebration. Anonymous activities have over the years leaned incoherently to the libertarian left and right, and everything in between, singling out everyone from Justin Bieber fans to feminists, fascists, cybersecurity specialists, and engaged in the kind of pervert-exposing vigilantism that blue-collar tabloid readers have long been mocked for.

To understand the seemingly contradictory politics of 4chan, Anonymous and its relationship to the alt-right, it is important to remember that the gradual right-wing turn in chan culture centered around the politics board /pol/, as compared to the less overtly political but always extreme "random" board /b/. Along the way left-leaning "moral fags" who had gravitated toward AnonOps IRCs suffered from a degree of state spying and repression during the height of Anonymous's public profile from around 2010 to 2012. This absence of the more libertarian left-leaning element within chan culture created a vacuum in the image boards that the rightist side of the culture was able to fill with their expert style of anti-PC shock humor memes.

4chan began with users sharing Japanese anime, created by a teenage Chris Poole (aka moot) and based on the anime-sharing site 2chan. Poole's main influence for the style of the site was inspired by a Something Awful subforum known as the "Anime Death Tentacle Rape Whorehouse." It was set up in October 2003 and by 2011, it grew to around 750 million page views a month. New users were called newfags and older users oldfags. It became a massively influential and creative forum known for pranks, memes, and images that "cannot be unseen." The culture of the site was not only deeply and shockingly misogynist, but also self-deprecating in its own self-mockery of nerdish "beta" male identity. Cultural touchstones included war-based video games and films like *Fight Club* and *The Matrix*. There was no registration or login required, so posts were typically all under the username "Anonymous."

This culture of anonymity fostered an environment where the users went to air their darkest thoughts. Weird pornography, in-jokes, nerdish argot, gory images, suicidal, murderous, and incestuous thoughts, racism, and misogyny were characteristic of the environment created by this strange virtual experiment, but it was mostly funny memes. Poole has called 4chan a "meme factory" and it undoubtedly created countless memes that made their way into mainstream Internet-culture. The most famous early examples of these were probably LOLcats, a cat-picture based style of image macro, and rickrolling, the use of a link to seemingly serious content that sends its user to a video of Rick Astley singing "Never Gonna Give You Up."

The users of 4chan/b/ acted collectively on things like making Chris Poole person of the year in *Time* magazine's online poll in 2008 and the collective cyber bullying of a random eleven-year-old, Jessie Slaughter, in 2010. They got hold of her name and address, harassed her, and encouraged her to commit suicide after she made a silly video of herself speaking in gangsta-rap style. Her situation was, unsurprisingly, not improved by her father posting a video in defense of his upset daughter, in which he threatened to call the "cyberpolice." In their emotionally underdeveloped way, lack of Internet-culture knowledge is always license on 4chan for any level of cruelty. They also acted collectively on less sinister pranks like Operation Birthday Boy, when an elderly man posted an online ad saying: "people wanted for birthday party." Touched by the lonely old man's appeal, they found his name, address, and phone number, and sent him hundreds of birthday cards, and orders of cake and strippers.

In the *New York Times*, Mattathias Schwartz described 4chan/b/ like this:

The anonymous denizens of 4chan's other boards—devoted to travel, fitness and several genres of pornography—refer to the /b/-dwellers as "/b/tards." Measured in terms of depravity, insularity and traffic-driven turnover, the culture of /b/ has little precedent. /b/ reads like the inside of a highschool bathroom stall, or an obscene telephone party line, or a blog with no posts and all comments filled with slang that you are too old to understand.

A common reference on the alt-right "kek" started on 4chan and translated to "lol" in comment boards on the multiplayer videogame *World of Warcraft*, while Pepe the Frog, originating in Matt Furie's Web comic *Boy's Club*, epitomizes online in-joke meme humor. Kek is also an ancient Egyptian deity represented as a frog-headed man while "the Church of Kek" and "praise Kek" refer to their ironic religion.

One of the things that linked the often nihilistic and ironic chan culture to a wider culture of the alt-right orbit was their opposition to political correctness, feminism, multiculturalism, etc., and its encroachment into their freewheeling world of anonymity and tech. In the US, one of the early cases of orchestrated attacks against such encroaching women was aimed at Kathy Sierra, a tech blogger and journalist. Sierra had been the keynote speaker at South by Southwest Interactive and her books were top sellers. The backlash against her was sparked when she supported a call to moderate reader comments, which at the time was seen as undermining the libertarian hacker ethic of absolute Internet freedom, although it has since become standard. Commenters on her blog began harassing and threatening her en mass, making the now routine rape and death threats received by women like Sierra. Personal details about her family and home address were posted online and hateful responses included photoshopped images of her with a noose beside her head, a shooting target pointed at her face and a creepy image of her being gagged with women's underwear. The personalized backlash against her was so extreme that she felt she had to close down her blog and withdraw from speaking engagements. When she explained on her blog why she had to step back from public life, writing that she was terrified that her stalkers might go through with their threats, it sparked a whole new wave of geek hatred against her.

Andrew Auernheimer (aka weev), a now well-known hacker and troll, seems to have been heavily involved in the attacks against Sierra, spreading false information online about her being a battered wife and a former prostitute. In 2009, weev claimed to have hacked into Amazon's system and reclassified books about homosexuality as porn. Once a part of the Occupy movement, he now regularly posts anti-Semitic and anti-gay rants on YouTube, has a swastika tattoo on his chest, and was also the self-appointed president of a trolling initiative called the Gay Nigger Association of America. This was dedicated to opposing popular blogging and other mainstream activities, thought to be destroying authentic Internet-culture. Sierra has commented on how things have progressed: "What happened to me pales in comparison to what's happening to women online today… I thought things would get better. Mostly, it's just gotten worse."

Although online spaces and comment sections had started to develop a shocking level of woman-hatred years before, one of the early mainstream discussions of online misogynist extremism was sparked when Helen Lewis interviewed feminist writers in the *New Statesman*, who brought to light some of what they experienced. Feminist blogger and activist Cath Elliot wrote:

> If I'd been trying to keep a tally I would have lost count by now of the number of abusive comments I've received since I first started writing online back in 2007. And by abusive I don't mean comments that disagree with whatever I've written—I came up through the trade union movement don't forget, and I've worked in a men's prison, so I'm not some delicate flower who can't handle a bit of banter or heated debate—no, I'm talking about personal, usually sexualized abuse, the sort that on more than one occasion now has made me stop and wonder if what I'm doing is actually worth it. […] I read about how I'm apparently too ugly for any man to want to rape, or I read graphic descriptions detailing precisely how certain implements should be shoved into one or more of my various orifices.

Feminist blogger Dawn Foster wrote:

> The worst instance of online abuse I've encountered happened when I blogged about the Julian Assange extradition case. [...] Initially it was shocking: in the space of a week, I received a rabid email that included my home address, phone number and workplace address, included as a kind of threat. Then, after tweeting that I'd been waiting for a night bus for ages, someone replied that they hoped I'd get raped at the bus stop.

Feminist sex writer Petra Davis later wrote:

> When I started getting letters at my flat, I reported them to the police, but they advised me to stop writing provocative material. Eventually, I was sent an email directing me to a website advertising my services as a sex worker, with my address on the front page under the legend "fuck her till she screams, filth whore, rape me all night cut me open," and some images of sexually mutilated women. It was very strange, sitting quietly in front of my screen looking at those images, knowing that the violence done to these other women was intended as a lesson ... Of course, it didn't take long to take the site down, but by then I was thoroughly sick of the idea and more or less stopped writing about sex from any perspective.

Significant here is yet another cross-pollinating section of the broader alt-right milieu—masculinist and neomasculinist antifeminist online subcultures. These are typically concerned with the decline of Western masculinity and some advocate things like the male separatism of Men Going Their Own Way (MGTOW), while others advise a more aggressive style of social-Darwinian informed pick-up artistry to "game" the human system. But it was really the broadest orbit of the alt-right, which became known as the alt-light, that popularized this new diffuse and chaotic online set of cross-pollinating subcultures and helped bring it into the mainstream. These included social media celebrity figures like Milo,

Twitter, and blogging stars like Mike Cernovich, who wrote the male assertiveness guide *Gorilla Mindset*, former *Vice* editor Gavin McInnes, and a host of Pepe meme-making gamers and 4chan-style shitposters, who had little in the way of a coherent commitment to conservative thought or politics but shared an anti-PC impulse and a common aesthetic sensibility. What we now call the alt-right is really this collection of lots of separate tendencies that grew semi-independently but which were joined under the banner of a bursting forth of anti-PC cultural politics through the culture wars of recent years. The irreverent trolling style associated with 4chan grew in popularity in response to the expanding identity politics of more feminine spaces like Tumblr. This, itself, spilled over eventually into "real life" in the ramping up of campus politics around safe spaces and trigger warnings, "gamergate," and many other battles.

One can feel the life draining out of the body at the thought of retelling or rereading the story of the gamergate controversy, one which involved internal controversies, hit pieces, hate campaigns, splits and a level of sustained high emotion more fitting for a response to a genocide than a spat over videogames. But for the sake of introduction here is a synopsis, which will undoubtedly satisfy neither side. In the lead-up to the gamergate controversy, feminist games critic Anita Sarkeesian found herself at the receiving end of a hate campaign like the Sierra case, but this time involving hundreds of thousands of participants and a level of vitriol utterly baffling to those outside of the gaming world, which lasted for several years. Her offense was creating a series of YouTube videos introducing viewers to some elementary concepts from feminist media criticism in an accessible and pretty mild-mannered style. Her level of criticism, as a self-identified games fan and someone who sought to reform rather than censor games, would be considered quite normal in literary or film criticism. These other audiences and critics are used to debate and to a relatively civilized adult kind of discourse, in which one can describe an old Hollywood classic as sexist without doubting its aesthetic value and one can disagree without going straight to the rape and death threats. Her videos feature no calls for video games to be censored or banned. They also offer no criticisms more harsh than what you might read from other pop-culture critics like Charlie

Brooker or Mark Kermode on some very obviously retrograde depictions of women in *some* video games.

For this intolerable crime, Sarkeesian has endured years of jaw-droppingly dark and disturbing personal abuse. Typical online commentary has included things like: "I'll rape you and put your head on a stick," "It would be funny if five guys raped her right now," "I violently masturbate to your face" and the old 4chan standard "Tits or get the fuck out." Her Wikipedia page was vandalized with pornographic images and hateful messages. There was also a campaign to mass report all of her social media accounts as spam, fraud or even terrorism.

Attempts were made to hack her website through a distributed denial of service (DDoS) attack and to hack into her email. Pornographic images of her being raped by video game characters were created and one offended male gamer even created a video game in which players could punch Anita's face until it was bloodied and bruised, and her eyes blackened and swollen. If you look up Anita today on YouTube you'll find countless videos devoted to hating her and obsessively trying to destroy her reputation and career. This was largely based on the fact that she ran a Kickstarter campaign that made more money than initially planned precisely because of the harassment. All of this was done, remember, to prove that sexism was *definitely not*, as she had so outrageously claimed, an issue in the "gaming community." Tactics such as DDoS and doxxing (exposing the person's personal details to enable their mass harassment) used by 4chan and originating in Usenet culture became central to attacks by the anti-feminist gamers. Games marketed to the antifeminist gamergate audience were more likely to aestheticize war, violence, and technology, while in the years preceding gamergate, the market for games directed at women had grown. This was especially so with games like *Candy Crush*, aimed at teenage girls who don't know what *World of Warcraft* is and which obviously offended those who considered themselves real gamers. Gamergate itself kicked off when Zoe Quinn created a video game called *Depression Quest*, which even to a non-gamer like me looked like a terrible game, featuring many of the fragility- and mental-illness-fetishizing characteristics of the kind of feminism that has emerged online in recent years.

It was the kind of game, about depression, that would have worked as a perfect parody of everything the gamergaters hated about SJWs (social justice warriors).

Nevertheless, her dreadful game got positive reviews from politically sympathetic indie games journalists, which turned into a kind of catalyst for the whole gamergate saga. It was understood to be either a war over ethics in games journalism or an excuse to attack feminists and women entering the gamer world, depending on whom you ask. First, let me be clear on my own position on gaming. If you're an adult, I think you should probably be investing your emotional energies elsewhere. And that includes feminist gaming, which has always struck me as being about as appealing as feminist porn; in other words, not at all. However, anyone with some grasp on the basic norms of human conduct will still be able to see why the fallout was utterly unhinged based on Quinn's bad game, other cases of alleged biased reviews and what was no doubt an ideological project to change gaming to make some of it more feminist-friendly. It became possibly the biggest flame war in the history of the Internet so far, an overreaction on a grand scale, in which everyone accused everyone else of lying and malicious intent.

Eron Gjoni, Quinn's ex-boyfriend, posted on forums that she had cheated on him, setting off a wave of attacks on her in which she claims her haters began sending revenge porn to her family and employers, and trying to hack her accounts. Quinn was, needless to say, threatened with rape and death, and was doxxed. They then attacked a series of feminist gamers and games critics, who waded in, including Brianna Wu, Felicia Day and Jennifer Allaway. In each case there are countless conflicting accounts about the nature of threats and attacks, but even taking the uncontroversial ones alone, it is fair to say they did receive a level of abuse that in the pre-Internet days were reserved for few others than child murderers. This got so out of hand that even the founder of 4chan and champion of the anonymous Internet, moot, banned gamergate talk from 4chan, eventually causing him to leave the site, and the gamergaters moved to the more lawless 8chan.

Quinn found and recorded some of the conversations that took place on a 4chan IRC called "burgersandfries" in which users conspired to destroy her career using the most extreme misogynist language and motivations. In this chat, they express their hatred and disgust toward her, and their glee at the thought of ruining her career. They also expressed fantasies about her being raped and killed. They hoped all the harassment would drive her to suicide and only the thought of 4chan getting bad publicity in response convinced some of them that this isn't something they should hope for. They distributed falsified nude pictures of her, posting links to online archives of them and sending them to Quinn's supporters. They attempted to dig up information about her family and to track down anyone with links to her. One found a picture of Quinn at age thirteen and posted a link to it. So committed were they to ethics in games journalism that in this discussion they discuss Quinn's vagina as "wide," large enough to "fit 12 dicks at once," and "a festering cheesefilled vagina" that leaves "a trail of cunt slime" wherever she goes and then speculated about its smell.

Jenn Frank, an award-winning freelance games journalist, wrote an article entitled "How to Attack a Woman Who Works in Video Gaming" for the *Guardian* that looked at on-going harassment. It outlined the ways in which trolls were harming women who work in the male-dominated field:

> Someone recently and bafflingly tried to hack into my email and phone contacts. This is all very frightening to write, and so I must disclose that I am biased, insofar as I am terrified. I have worked in this industry for most of the last nine—not always perfect—years and I have never professed to be a perfect person. However, my values, my belief that abuse must not, cannot become "normal," "acceptable" or "expected" is at odds with *oh, God, please, why are they doing this, what's the point, don't let it be me, don't let it be me.* My unabashed love for video games, my colleagues and my work have a conflict of interest with my own terror.

Games writer Jennifer Hepler also came under attacks, in which she claims to have been sent hundreds of abusive messages on Twitter, calling her things like an "obese cunt" and threatening her. Feminist gamers complained that games writer Felicia Day was publicly dismissed as a "booth babe" by a male games journalist. Games designer Patricia Hernandez drew the attention of 4chan, when she called it a "cathedral of misogyny." *Encyclopedia Dramatica* has a permanent entry for the memes 4chan created inspired by her comment, where she is described as:

> A fat, wetback "game journalist" with sausage fingers and a chin like Jay Leno who works for Kotaku, a gaming gossip site infamous for allowing game designers to sleep with its columnists for good reviews and publicity. Patricia is a noted lesbian and feminazi who follows in Kotaku's proud tradition of writing countless articles about how various games either promote rape or literally rape their female players. Another staple of Kotaku "journalism" she takes part in is nepotism, which explains why every other article to come from her chubby hands is about her live-in girlfriend.

Without getting too far into the minutiae, and at this point it would be impossible to reach the end of all the various accusations of lies and contestations of how the mass event unfolded, the important feature of the furor here is the role it played in uniting different online groups and in spreading the tactics of chan culture to the broad online right. Gamergate brought gamers, rightist chan culture, anti-feminism and the online far right closer to mainstream discussion and it also politicized a broad group of young people, mostly boys, who organized tactics around the idea of fighting back against the culture war being waged by the cultural left. These included all kinds of people from critics of political correctness to those interested in the overreach of feminist cultural crusades. These brought into the fold people like Christina Hoff Sommers, the classical liberal who started a video series called *The Factual Feminist*, which aimed to expose faulty statistics within feminism. Somewhere in the mix with the polite and light-hearted Sommers were also apolitical gamers, *South Park* conservatives, 4channers, hardline anti-feminists, and young people in the process of moving to the political far right without any of the moral baggage of conservatism. It also made Milo's ill-fated career, as he used it to shoot to mainstream celebrity status. Ultimately, the gamergaters were correct in their perception that a revived feminist movement was trying to change the culture and this was the front, their beloved games, that they chose to fight back on. The battle has since moved on to different issues with increasingly higher stakes, but this was the galvanizing issue that drew up the battle lines of the culture wars for a younger online generation.

The culture of 4chan, Anonymous etc., in the pre-gamergate days of Occupy and Anonymous could have gone another way. Long before this "geeks vs. feminists" battle, the libertarian left had its own pro-hacker, pro-computer geek, Internet-centric political tradition, which some in the early Anonymous milieu obviously drew influence from. Hakim Bey's idea of the temporary autonomous zone was based on what he called "pirate utopias," and he argued that the attempt to form a permanent culture or politics inevitably deteriorates into a structured system that stifles individual creativity. His language and ideas influenced anarchism and later, online cultures that advocated illegal downloading, anonymity, hacking and experiments like bitcoin. Echoes of John Perry Barlow's manifesto "A Declaration of the Independence of Cyberspace" can be seen in this earlier period of Anon culture and in analyses that reflect a more radical horizontalist politics, like Gabriella Coleman's work. Barlow was one of the founders of the Electronic Frontier Foundation, anarchist hackers and defenders of an Internet free of state intervention, capitalist control and monopolizing of the online world. In a similar style to the rhetoric of 4chan and Anonymous ("we are legion"), it warned:

> Governments of the Industrial World, you weary giants of flesh and steel, I come from Cyberspace, the home of Mind. On behalf of the future I ask you of the past to leave us alone. You are not welcome among us. You have no sovereignty where we gather.

Instead, this leaderless anonymous online culture ended up becoming characterized by a particularly dark preoccupation with thwarted or failed white Western masculinity as a grand metaphor, which has had some "real-life" manifestations. On 4chan a post, dated October 1, 2015, read:

> The first of our kind has struck fear into the hearts of America ... This is only the beginning. The Beta Rebellion has begun. Soon, more of our brothers will take up arms to become martyrs to this revolution.

The dramatic and knowingly cinematic tone was typical of the online style that hides itself from interpretation through a postmodern tonal distance, so that if any normie were to interpret it literally they would be laughed at. But in this case it was referring to the real news that a young man named Chris Harper-Mercer had killed nine classmates and injured nine others before shooting himself at Umpqua Community College in Roseburg, Oregon. The night before the shooting, a post on 4chan's /r9k/ board warned fellow commenters from the northwestern United States to steer clear of school that day. The first responder in the thread asked: "Is the beta uprising finally going down?," while others encouraged the anonymous poster and gave him tips on how to conduct a mass shooting.

In 2014, an anonymous 4chan user submitted several photos of what appeared to be a woman's naked and strangled corpse, along with a confession:

> Turns out it's way harder to strangle someone to death than it looks on the movies ... Her son will be home from school soon. He'll find her then call the cops. I just wanted to share the pics before they find me. I bought a bb gun that looks realistic enough. When they come, I'll pull it and it will be suicide by cop. I understand the doubts. Just check the fucking news. I have to lose my phone now.

Police later announced that the victim, Amber Lynn Coplin, was the woman in the photo. Her boyfriend, David Michael Kalac, was arrested after a brief police chase and charged with murder. If further proof that the anti-PC taboo-breaking culture of 4chan is not just "for the lulz" is needed, after the November 2015 shooting of five Black Lives Matter protesters in Minneapolis, a video emerged of two of the men involved, wearing balaclavas and driving to a Black Lives Matter protest, saying: "We just wanted to give everyone a heads up on /pol/ … Stay white."

Just a few years ago the left-cyberutopians claimed that "the disgust had become a network" and that establishment old media could no longer control politics, that the new public sphere was going to be based on leaderless user-generated social media. This network has indeed arrived, but it has helped to take the right, not the left, to power. Those on the left who fetishized the spontaneous leaderless Internet-centric network, declaring all other forms of doing politics old hat, failed to realize that the leaderless form actually told us little about the philosophical, moral, or conceptual content of the movements involved. Into the vacuum of "leaderlessness" almost anything could appear. No matter how networked, "transgressive," social media savvy or non-hierarchical a movement may be, it is the content of its ideas that matter just as much as at any point in history, as Evgeny Morozov cautioned at the time. The online environment has undoubtedly allowed fringe ideas and movements to grow rapidly in influence and while these were left leaning it was tempting for politically sympathetic commentators to see it as a shiny new seductive shortcut to transcending our "end of history." What we've since witnessed instead is that this leaderless formation can express just about any ideology even, strange as it may seem, that of the far right.

This essay is a reprint of "The Leaderless Digital Counter-Revolution," in Angela Nagle, *Kill All Normies: Online Culture Wars from 4Chan and Tumblr to Trump and the Alt-Right* (London: Zero Books, 2017).

So Heavy Grasshoppers:
Allochthonous Notes on Populism

Benjamin H. Bratton

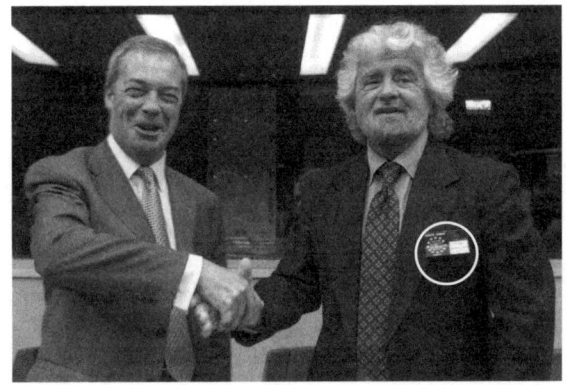

We began planning The New Normal program at the Strelka Institute in Moscow in the summer of 2016, deep in the thick of the United States presidential election cycle. As you will recall— way back then—populist storms swirled in many directions at once, some progressive, some reactionary, and many that did not fit neatly along the Left/Right linear spectrum. Post-Brexit but Pre-Trump, I wrote:

> In the exact spot where a viable future should be, something insufferably backwards fills it in: a psychotic simulation of medieval geopolitics burning as bright as creepy clown hair. The rise of ethno-nationalist Populism is a global phenomenon with global causes. Yet in each case, locals either blame or congratulate themselves for their unique failure/accomplishment. But from Manila to Milwaukee, we see the same demographic voting

patterns of urban highly-educated cosmopolitans and rural less-educated monocultural nationalists (and/or national monoculturalists). Even as globalization has delinked class from geography in uneven ways, we try to deal with the phenomenon one 18th century jurisdiction at a time. And yet this is also when networks of city-states seem decisively detached from their national hosts. For those from "district 13" in our real-life *Hunger Games*, the city is a source of arbitrary power and in this way, is urbanization itself a focus of the populist backlash?

Now mid-Trump and pre-Who Knows What, it is worth unpacking this a bit and considering the consolidated gains, however fragile, of right populism more generally. What do we mean by "Populism"? What is it *not*, what are the real alternatives to its "autistic" narrowing of the political spectrum? At a moment when all polities are forced to choose, less between feckless bureaucrat A or B than between actual literal clowns, we can ask: for how much longer?[1]

I should admit that from an analytic perch I don't make as sharply-cut distinctions between Left and Right modes of large-scale capital "P" Populist movements as some others might. This is not because I can't distinguish between their goals or worldviews, or don't acknowledge that politics is predicated on deep structural antagonisms, but because the means/ends dynamics of Populist genres of political drama and mobilization are poorly suited to the situations at which they are aimed. Characteristic correspondences between Left and Right Populisms are well-understood in mainstream political science. *For*: the people, common sense, a fair deal, economic isolationism, simplicity, folk aesthetics, inspirational and affective politics, appeals to community, immediacy, etc. *Against*: the establishment, global elites, technocratic expertise, degenerate abstraction, economic complexity, liberalism, incremental compromises, etc. *(Sometimes) a fondness for*: conspiracy theories, easy redistribution, xenophobic suspicion, big schemes, cults of personality, etc. The best cure for Right Populism is (likely) not Left Populism, especially as they are not as easily distinguished as they seem from the inside. This does not, however, exclude Left (small "p") populism from effective responses and tactics, nor mean that Populist movements can be reduced to type in form or content. It is simply to say that more Populism is not more better; we seek a way around their shoddy impasses.

Crucially, the diversity of political positions is not represented by the friend/enemy divides that may animate particular Populist movements. Many Right and Left Populists mobilize declarations of "war" (of "self-defense") against the opposite side according to how it imagines a linear spectral continuum (red versus black, black versus red), but we can't help but see that they often have much more in common with one another than they do with other positions and programs. This may simply repeat Horseshoe theory by which extreme Left and extreme Right politics bend around the spectrum and converge (a notion that also demonstrates the "argument to moderation" fallacy), and in other ways it confirms how a mimetic necessity to narrativize political complexity takes on a life all its own, as it may for any politics. Still, the cartography of differences that are drawn by Populist movements to define their own purposes and goals are extremely unreliable guides to the actual differences of possible positions among the agonistic field of a larger political territory. Excluded is not just a vast "middle" of the spectrum caught between two poles, but all positions that can never be covered by a straight line drawn over a deep volume, which is to say most positions. Perhaps the harm is that under the guise of popular inclusiveness, Populism actually reduces and narrows the range of all political articulation to only the remedial vocabularies with which it is capable.

In response to the invited theme of this volume, I will attempt to put one pin on the board regarding the role of nativism, traditional national geography in (mostly) right-wing populism as part of a broader reaction to globalization's disembedding tendencies (not a remotely novel observation) and do so on behalf of an anti-nativist, non-autochonous geopolitics (which I will not have space to properly articulate below). That is, among the most obvious and pernicious imaginaries of right-wing populism are delusional nativist racism, tribalism and nationalism that translate into spatial pogroms both speculative and realized. A decisive alternative, predicated on fundamental openness, understands that humans are a mobile species. Moving out of Africa, more than once, and eventually across the Alaskan straits for example, "we" are the ultimate invasive species. Even before agricultural settlement, humans built massive land-works that oriented semi-nomadic groups. Sometimes the lines drawn were exclusive borders and sometimes they were paths of flight. Over the course of time, as ecosystems shift between temporary states of equilibrium and disruption, the same places are occupied by different humans in *waves*, some very slow and some much faster.

In this specific sense, "indigeneity" is always relational; one thing is comparatively indigenous to something else and its autochthonous adaptations are is always conditional. Obviously the plasticity of the term belongs to the myriad heterogeneous Indigenous cultures who encountered, were brutalized by and/or resisted historically modern colonialism, but in another sense, the term could define adaptations that appear in a given location in correspondence with others sited there, and so would include cultures that are indigenous to industrial and post-industrial society.[2] They have their own mythologies. Where the forest is made of metal, plastic and electricity, many hold that the extraction and vaporization of fossil fuels has no cumulative negative effect on the whole of the machinic forest. This is not just a belief; it is essential to their ontology. Such magical thinking allows them to keep their rituals and festivals intact. However when "indigeneous" is deployed to mean grounded emplacement, authentic belonging, interior durability, and spooky interconnectedness, then such a terribly modern mobilization of the concept is all too compatible with reactionary movements that misrecognize the diversity of ways to situate human culture as some naturalized Tolkienesque ethnozoology.[3] With caveats, we observe that today's anti-globalist ethnonationalist Populist qualifies as another kind of politics of "indigeneity": a symptomatic blowback from post-colonial demographic flows, the transnational network effects of financial platforms, and the inevitable provincialization of North American and European experience as it shifts off the center of global history. Drawing gross parallels between divergent notions of indigeneity based in different relations to colonial history is not to conflate them, but given humans' shared (and also divergent) migrancy, when apparently unlike notions arrive at symmetrical irredentist claims on the present it suggests that one version is an inadequate solution for another.

Below is a scan of some recent encounters. In Russia—where I spend a lot of time of late—the valor of patriotic nativism is claimed forcefully by many Rightists, such as Alexander Dugin, as an explicitly anti-Western and anti-Modern bulwark of mystic Eurasian Traditionalism. Dugin is a sometimes Putin-whisperer (and perhaps another weird Sarkov project), an evangelist of Heidegger and Schmitt, and writes extensively about how much inspiration is to be taken takes from these "grounded" anti-modern philosophical projects.[4] Like filmmaker Nikita Mikhalkov, his theories echo well with his audience's geopolitical folklore, such as the Dulles Plan, the purported American long-standing masterplan to undermine Russian culture with pernicious and invasive cultural degradation.[5] In the USA, Russian communism once played a similar role as the undermining external (((Other))), and today this feud amplifies the infamy of election-hacking trolls (as real as they are). In Serbia, a long, long-standing European mythic irredentist nationalism calls on battles fought long before the colonial era in the Americas. Talk to any Le Pen/Front National supporter in France (or closer by, your colleagues' Alain de Benoist books on their shelves) and soon enough you will hear appeals to *Français de souche* or the "indigenous French" to validate their program. Meanwhile, out on the American prairie at Standing Rock, the Lakota draw upon rights of ancestral occupation to block a pipeline of carbon from Canadian tar sands into the planetary greenhouse, withstanding considerable martial brutality and tolerating weeks upon weeks of drum circles, solidarity check-ins, and patronizing exoticization. On the expansive far side of suburban sprawl in Nevada, the very old and very white Cliven Bundy drawls his own confused "original claim" to his multi-generational inherited plot of grazing land, and does so with anti-cosmopolitan notions familiar to Dugin.

In the service of Populism, the work that the concept of indigeneity does is relative and uneven because the intersecting experiences of war and empire, colonialist and otherwise, offer no single line to measure it. Still, one can't evangelize a politico-cultural program based on a core scenario of place-based native communities with trans-scientific bonds of soil, water, blood, food, language, religion, all organized by a strongly policed identity, and menaced by global, liberal technocratic foreign elites, etc. and not also hear how well this rhymes with *Alternative für Deutschland*. But that dynamic is clearly not the only axis on which the term rotates. Indigeneity is also planetary; humans are indigenous to our own movement and dislocation. Migration is our habitat because it allows things to combine and break apart; now we may fashion identities that prioritize mobility and migration as unexceptional, being-at-home in our dislocations: ours is to *become allochthonous*.

While affective expressions of sovereignty (representations of self-mastery, dignification and solidarity, etc.) can be their own reward, they also animate structural vacillations—both coherent and incoherent—between wall-building self-encapsulation and expansive mobilization. Even assuming that arcs of hominid migration are unstoppable, other than by the most extreme means, we recognize that borders do not only cleave but, like all interfaces, perform a generative function as well. Island ecologies produce unique species. The membranes of any assemblage cohere and incorporate bodies through inclusion as much as exclusion, but which bodies and why so? Which designs on interiorization versus exteriorization matter most for the future of political geography? We observe both secessionist withdrawal into traditional territories as well as consolidations of much larger swaths into hemispherical stacks; we see the continuing expansions of the *de facto* sovereignties of cloud platforms as well as the reformation of traditional States into regional cloud platforms.

What near-term developments are likely? Perhaps through more radical abstractions of sovereignty we can anticipate States largely depopulated of people. Such jurisdictions of convenience may look like robotic port cities along the Arctic Sea or like Syria, where Assad seems to have sorted out that he doesn't actually need a population in order to have a country. It may prove easier for him not to have civilians at all, just pay an army to protect the sovereign wealth of industrial resources without the nuisance of a larger society. The living corollary of such empty legal entities

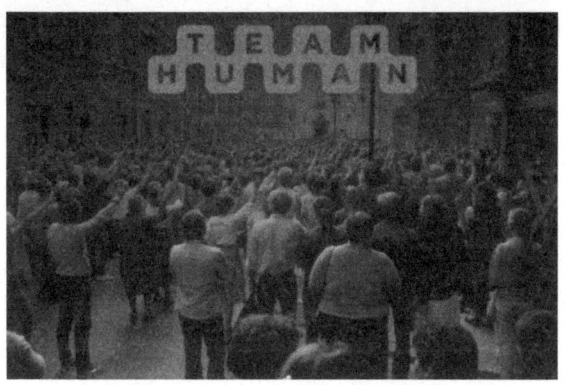

may be the informal shadow economies which by some estimates count for as much as one fifth of the global economy. The former is a state economy without people, the latter is a social economy without a state, both dark and probably mutually dependent circumventions of the order of things.

Some novelties which appear initially interesting for one reason, but which prove uninteresting for another, may yet prove important for other reasons still. When Denmark's Digital Ambassador suggests that his country's relations with Google are as important as with other States, we shouldn't smirk too hard, nor take this as necessarily bad news. Blockchains could be or should be interesting if they open up the economic user position beyond Lockean individualism, not because they refortify its illusions (and yet …). Estonia's e-residency program may be interesting not because it allows you to pay taxes to Baltic states you have never visited, but because it suggests that there is no imperative link between the distributed provision of state social services and legacy state jurisdictions. The geographic walls that sort citizens from a wilderness of non-citizens may become taller and wider but less and less necessary; formal state citizenship itself could be as mobile as it wants to be. This may prove important, for example, to any broad-based universal basic income (UBI) scheme, especially any based on Pigovian taxes, because there is a danger that as wealthy liberal jurisdictions offer this baseline dividend, the prophylactic divisions between who is *in* and who is *out* will be more stark, portending transgenerational partitions of tiered levels of citizenship.[6] In March of this year Italy's Five Star Movement peddled its version of UBI as part of a fuzzy Italians First platform. The cascading impacts of automation on various labor sectors and the people that comprise them may lead to ameliorative dividends (such as UBI) but may also harden the distinctions between formal citizens inside the border who would receive such payments and those on the outside looking in who would not. Instead of alleviating extreme disparities of wealth and security, UBI misapplied as "welfare chauvinism" may lock them in and accelerate them.

    Genuine confusion and ambivalence over the political, legal, and philosophical status of automation, robotics, and A.I. should inspire fewer calls for a normative "rehumanization" and more recognition and invention of the agency of irregular and non-anthropomorphic systems, carbon-based, and otherwise. Estonia has its Kratt Laws and everyone else can conjure their own versions.[7] Instead we sit through doomsaying professional trolls, yelling at the Cloud, and calling for a "nationalization of datacenters" as their "solutionist" remedy to abuses of data production and gathering, as if Chinese and Russian examples are not relevant. Also on the playlist are meme-chasing, tide-riding journalists promoting "Team Human" campaigns, taking an already problematic notion of human rights on a diluted reactionary turn toward resentful connotations of species privilege. Head for the door. What some call "techno-optimism" is rightly criticized for breathlessly positive investments of faith in quick technological fixes to complex conditions and painful histories, while Populist movements, in their most garish forms, exhibit a similar "impatience of revolutionaries," and offer instead equally-breathless quick political fixes.

    For our own *Grasshopper Lies Heavy* moment, States trade on dubious historical claims—geographic, ethnic, linguistic, etc.—in order to enforce new influence on land and in the Cloud.[8] The amalgamation of States' vertical integration and the cloud's power law dynamic is steering toward fundamentalist sovereignties and a narrowing of the political discourse, but not of the underlying spectrum of positions that could be articulated. This outcome is not inevitable; this vision of how things work is inaccurate, and so vulnerable. It holds that entities exist *first* as things, as bodies situated, and *then* interaction among those parts may ensue, this way or that (this misapprehension is also held, for different reasons, by some OOO[9] acolytes). For this view, internal relations of a social body precede, in time and value, any external and transitive relations that the polity may "enter into" in some adjacent and subsequent place. Instead, we should see the productive function of membranes to give shape and form, to draw exit and entrance, to compose differentiation and polypolarity of cultures already in motion. We would spend less time attending to an overdetermined placefulness than to the trophic cascades of discontiguous polities located not one location at a time but across sites and situations, across oceans and between molecules (with real atmospheric effects).

This reactionary moment also stems, as suggested, from an inability of "the West" to account for the entropic forces that it helped set in motion but which have now less need of its privileged steerage. It is like a cell whose walls have burst and which now swims in its own osmatic churn. We need to be very careful with the descriptions we use and should assume that neologisms may be in order. Some call the predicament "proto-fascist" but I find this imprecise and disappointingly Eurocentric, once again mistaking the local particular past for the global or unknowable future. Does over-employing the F word presume that *Europe's* past is the default measure for everyone else's future? It is the best term if you think Europe is actually the Center of History and that history is a closed-loop; not for just any eternal return but quite a particular one? Instead we might ask, for what does Xi Jinping's consolidations of power count? In what way is he and is he not a Populist? That is, what is coming next may be *horrible*, authoritarian and catastrophic, but it will not be necessarily Western in character. Decisively delinking Universalism from its European vernaculars — a real provincialization of Europe — is something the Left can find as difficult to fathom as the Right, though for different reasons.

I suspect (and hope) that the current wave of consolidation around legacy territories is a transitional interruption of the longer arc toward a more integrated planetary society. In whatever form "we" take, humans are and should remain a migratory species. Territories defined by very recent genomic occupation and/or divine archaeology (and vice versa) can be fortified, but to what end? In the coming years the discontiguous megaterritories that consolidate alternative sovereign domains, including hemispherical stacks, hold the potential for Galapagos Effects that may force new paths of productive diversification and new bridges, passages and teeming avenues between them. Finally leaving the 20th century, I prefer to see them as another episode of anthropogenic integration, not as its meltdown.

1
I hereby make the obligatory reference to the 2007 film *Idiocracy*, written and directed by University of California, San Diego alumnus, Mike Judge.

2
The term "Indigenous" is contested and changing: for some it is itself a figure of state violence, for others an identification of resistance to that violence, for others an important legal status through which land rights claimed can be adjudicated. For some discussion of its legal and political connotations see "The Concept of Indigeneity," in *Social Anthropology* (2006): 1, 14, 17–32. A multi-author debate on Alan Kuper's article critical of the renewed use of the term "indigenous": "The Return of the Native," *Current Anthropology* 44, no. 3 (2003). See also Guillermo Delgado and John Brown Childs, eds., *Indigeneity: Collected Essays* (New Pacific Press, 2012), and Francesca Merlan, "Indigeneity: Global and Local," *Current Anthropology* 50, no. 3 (2009): 303–33.

3
Consider, however obliquely, the scene at Camp Hobbit Fairs fairs in Italy in 1977, where, according to this author, a nascent far right merged *The Lord of the Rights* fandom with Julius Evola and Woodstock. See John Last, "How 'Hobbit Camps' Rebirthed Italian Fascism," *Atlas Obscura*, October 3, 2017, (https://www.atlasobscura.com/articles/hobbit-camps-fascism-italy.). The neo-Creationist notion that cultures and communities are situated and permanent, is derided by Michael Moorcock in this same article: "In Tolkien, everyone's in their place and happy to be there. We go there and back, to where we started. There's no escape, nothing will ever change and nobody will ever break out of this well-ordered world."

4
Dugin, "who's been described as everything from an occult fascist to a mystical imperialist, lost his prestigious job running the sociology department at Moscow State University in 2014 after activists accused him of encouraging genocide," is a one man Internet K-hole, so Google with caution. See Henry Meyer, Onur Ant, "Alexander Dugin: The One Russian Linking Donald Trump, Vladimir Putin and Recep Tayyip Erdogan," *The Independent*, February 3, 2017, Accessed November 01, 2018. http://www.independent.co.uk/news/world/americas/alexander-dugin-russian-academic-linking-us-president-donald-trump-vladimir-putin-turkey-president-a7560611.html. His rambling video essays against Transhumanism as a liberal plot are not to be missed. See "Prof. Alexander Dugin – Transhumanism," posted by "Hamza – Slay Your Dragon," YouTube video, September 18, 2016, 8:51, https://www.youtube.com/watch?v=dOw6unXjzaI. Vladislav Surkov came to some renown as a Kremlin simulationist in Metahaven's cinematic essay *The Sprawl* (2016). A collection of his essays is available on Amazon.

5
No American I have ever met has heard of the Dulles' Plan.

6
Pigovian tax seeks to correct for negative externalities and negative social costs brought about by a market transaction, such as pollution or obesity or climate change, etc.

7
"In Estonian mythology, a Kratt is a creature brought to life from hay or household objects." Proposed legislation to frame the legal status of artificial intelligence are called Kratt Laws. See this essay by the advisor of digital affairs for the Estonian government, Marten Kaevats, "Estonia Considers a 'Kratt Law' to Legalise Artificial Intelligence (AI)," *Medium*, https://medium.com/e-residency-blog/estonia-starts-public-discussion-legalising-ai-166cb8e34596.

8
In Philip K. Dick's *The Man in the High Castle* (1962), about a post-war era in which the United States is governed by the victorious German Nazi and Japanese Empire forces, *The Grasshopper Lies Heavy* is the title of a novel within a novel, authored by the character Hawthorne Abendsen. In Dick's novel the Axis powers won World War II but in *The Grasshopper* the alternative history is that the Allied powers won. For our world, the alternative reality in which Fascism actually did win after all seems not entirely unbelievable.

9
Object Oriented Ontology.

In the Name of God

Slavs & Tatars

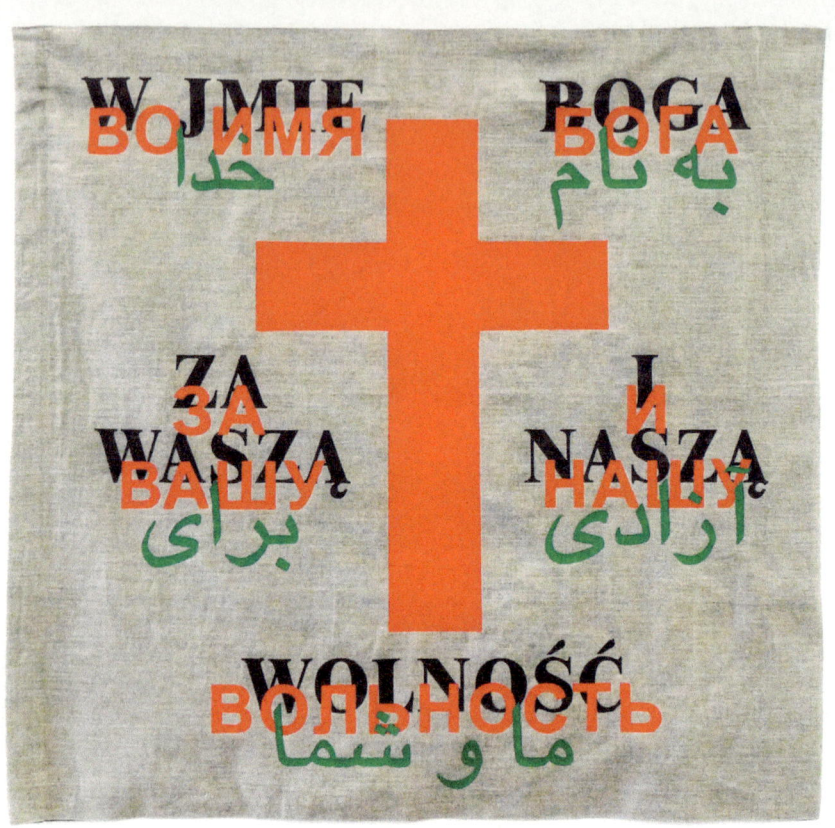

In the Name of God

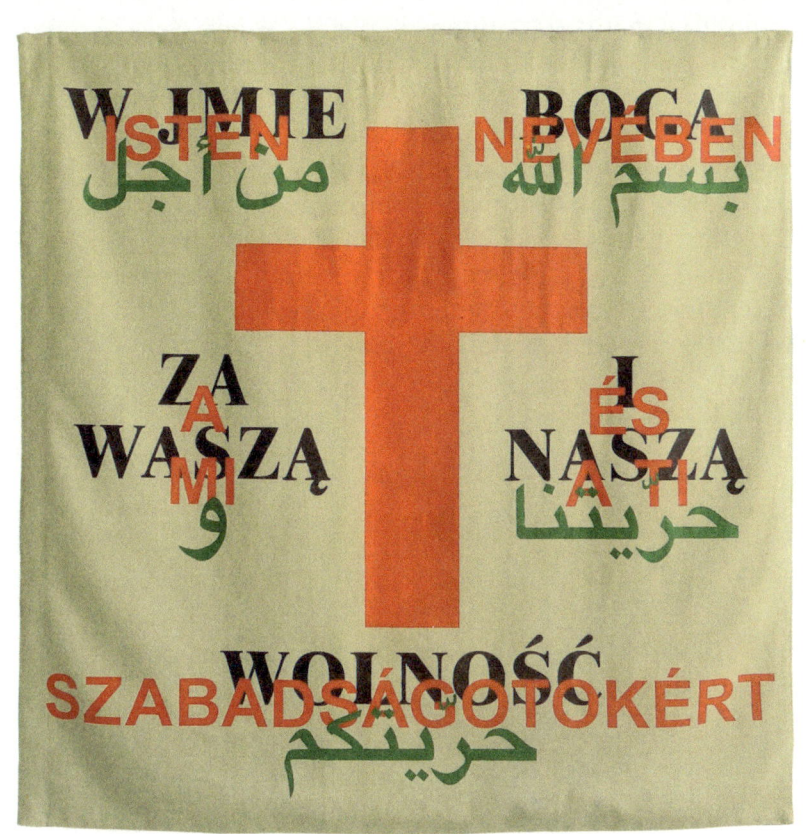

An unofficial motto of partitioned Poland, "W imię Boga za Naszą i Waszą Wolność" (In the Name of God, for Your Freedom and Ours), has been appropriated by peoples around the world in their struggles for self-determination. Featuring both Russian and Polish in its original iteration, the banner is a complex nod to the fate binding two countries whose history has been contentious to say the least. By translating the original into Persian and reinstating the Russian, *In the Name of God* addresses the transnational, if not transcendental nature of this phrase, aiming to rescue it from the jaws of parochial or imperial instrumentalization.

Slavs & Tatars
2018

Para–Platforms Symposium

Gothenburg, Sweden
November 25, 2017

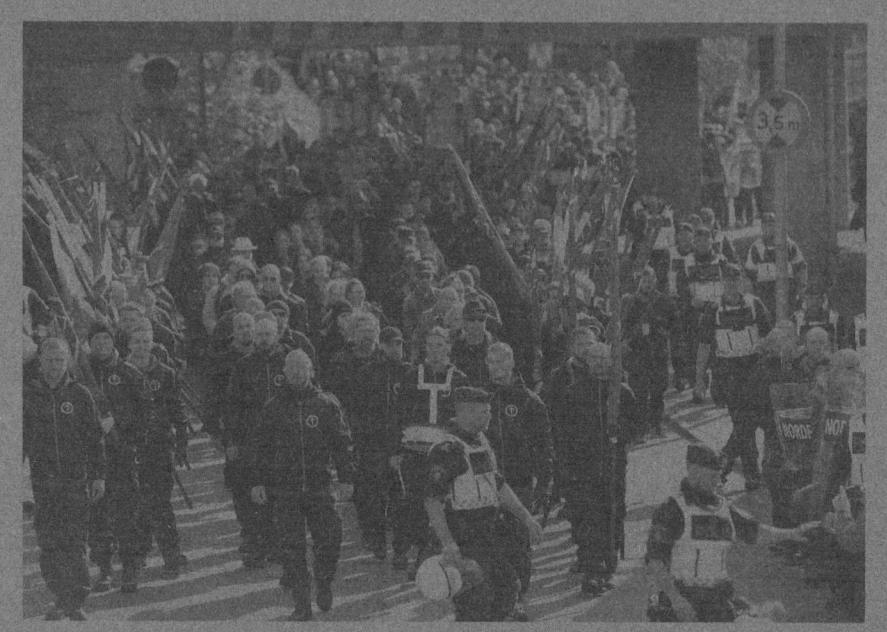

1

Introduction

Markus Miessen

This event is hosted by SPÄTI, our informal bar and central meeting space during the Design Festival, at this lovely bar co-organized by Studio NOCK. The event is also hosted by Design Politics, an extra-curricular content framework that I'm running together with Matthias Gunnarsson at HDK, the Academy of Design, here in Gothenburg.

The program this year is run under the umbrella issue of "cultures of assembly"—spaces of political assembly, and the design making and unmaking of those. In the context of this, one relevant question is that of popular political decision making, and the way in which populist politics and their spatial manifestations have been developing recently.

Some of you may not be so familiar with this particular image [fig.1] of a march by the Nordic Resistance, a Swedish, local phenomenon—a very well organized nationalist campaign here. Groups like the Nordic Resistance are an extreme case, but they use digitally-savvy media campaigns and new tech tools like those being used by other far-right groups—as Stephan Trüby and Hannes Grassegger will discuss. Meanwhile, Christina Varvia and Forensic Architecture have been researching the "Nationalsozialistischer Untergrund" (National Socialist Underground) phenomenon in Germany, as she will discuss, in part by working with equally if not more technologically sharp and emergent design tools.

So "Design Politics" in this context is the question of what design can or can not do. How is it misused in the context of politics? I've been working for some time on a particular interest in participation, and the way in which participation may be understood not as a romantic notion of inviting everyone around a table to make decisions together but as a more proactive mode of self-initiated practice. For me, what's very interesting is the question of how, as designers, we can get involved in questions of not only a given political environment, but also the way in which we develop tools that address consensus or dissensus, in terms of a productive mode of conflict that can be used to make decisions.

There's a very interesting and fitting German word which unfortunately translates very badly into English: *Einmischung*. Its meaning sits somewhere between the terms of proactive action and productive irritant. That's where you could say all of the three speakers are located and where their work and practices overlap. If one understands these three presentations as a set of approaches, there are some very exciting models to be witnessed and potentially deployed.

Without further delay: the three speakers today are Christina Varvia from Forensic Architecture, a London-based group of architects, artists and researchers; Hannes Grassegger, a Zurich-based economist and investigative journalist best known internationally for uncovering the relationship between Trump and Cambridge Analytica; and Stephan Trüby, architectural theorist and tireless researcher of right-wing spaces, currently a professor in Munich, but soon returning to the University of Stuttgart. Stephan and I, together with my studio in Berlin, are currently contributing to a major research project on spaces of right-wing populism which triggered this event today. That project initially started as a study on spaces mostly in the former East Germany, but what has now zoomed out and takes a European, and, with today's speakers in mind, even global perspective. I'd now like to invite Hannes Grassegger to open the symposium.

The Case of Trump & Brexit
Hannes Grassegger

Hi. Pleasure and honor to meet you all here in Gothenburg.

I'll be starting from a very left-wing space. Look at this beautiful photo of what Salvador Allende was planning to set up in socialist Chile in 1970: Project Cybersyn. [fig.2] It's a control room, a computerized operations center, for a planned economy. It's a cybernetic dream, which we've seen being realized only today—and which ended up in the hands of the Trump campaign.

  To better understand what a "control room" is: if you look back at all these computer-ish screens and buttons in the Cybersyn image, these seats were meant to orchestrate the Chilean economy and to have a central place from which the whole state could be managed. People in the control room would receive real-time information about the factors of the planning economy, like production numbers, where trucks are circulating, the flows of electricity etcetera, and be able to send back certain orders to elements within the economy. Tell the power station to pump out more energy in the South, for example. Try to circumvent a barred route via train-delivery. And so on. Actually, the people in the control room would do very little, but supervise and oversee the automated self-regulation of the system. Once necessary they would step in—hence the buttons and screens.

  This sort feedback loop is actually based on much older ideas, which started in the late 1940s. Just to show you how advances some of these ideas were, here's an essay of one of the founding fathers of cybernetics, Vannevar Bush. He developed the concept for this marvelous third eye, a kind of electronic goggle, which is probably the first draft of what later became Google

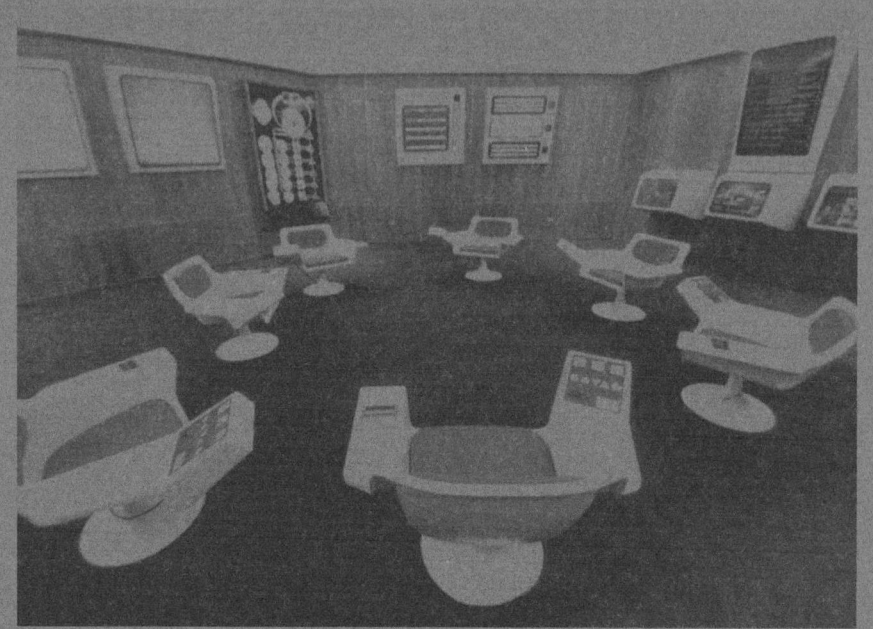

2

Industrial Design Group INTEC, Chile, 1971–1973

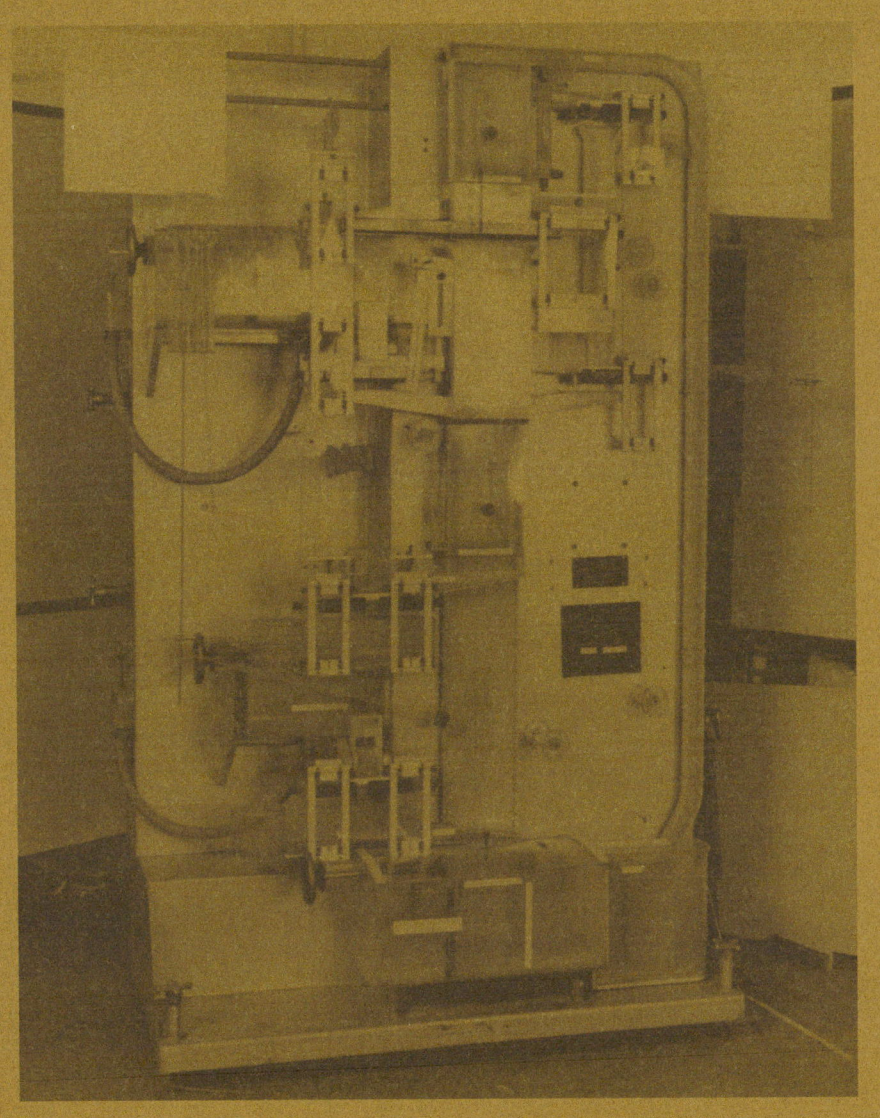

Glass. A lens that you put on your forehead that, once you read a scientific paper, would read the paper you are reading and then automatically sort through all the microfiche in an archive and see if there's something related in it which could be linked to what reading. So there were ideas like hypertext in the 1940s, already in place. The last image is an essay about the concept in the *Atlantic Magazine* in mid-1945. One of Bush's peers was Norbert Wiener, one of the founding fathers of cybernetics, author of the famous book *The Human Use of Human Beings* (1958).

The context of cybernetics is that during the late years of the Great War, scientists from different branches were brought together to develop methods on how the war could be won. Social scientists were brought together with engineers and technicians, and their big question was how to control a system that is part machine and part living being, meaning animal or man.

Cybernetics is the idea of controlling systems through technology, of, more precisely, steering a system with the help of feedback loops. The classic example to illustrate this is the thermostat. If you want to have the room temperature at twenty degrees, for example, you would set the room temperature there. The heating starts working and a thermometer in the thermostat discovers there's a difference of two degrees, and so it manages the heating system and lowers or increases the temperature. This is a feedback loop where you send a signal, receive information about the true state, then the system automatically adjusts.

Early on it was discovered that this could be used in social environments as well. Alban W. Phillips, an important economist in the late '40s, developed a machine that simulated the flows of money in the British economy. [fig.3] It's like an analog computer with a lot of liquid inside, and you can actually figure out the inflation rate and the amount of money circulating in the British economy. This is just one of the many examples where people started to apply these cybernetic ideas to manage more complex social systems.

While this is at the macro-level of society as an aggregate of human beings, at the very same time, within mathematics, psychology and economics, new methods were being developed to incentivize and influence the behavior of the individual being. This is Game Theory in particular. Then all of this came together in the late '60s, and in the cybernetic research environment a scientist named Stafford Beer was sent to Chile to help Allende kick start this great project Cybersyn, of "Let's apply cybernetic management structures to an economy." Unfortunately, this project failed terribly, not only because of the political situation, but mostly because the information infrastructure wasn't in place. At the time the Cybersyn control room was planned in 1971–73, it was meant to be connected to telegraph systems. The amount of time to get and send the information was actually overwhelming. It was basically a fancy futurist idea, because the data infrastructure wasn't there.

But today, in 2016–17, we all know the slogan: "Data is the new oil." Some even say "data is water," because it's so ubiquitous. Please note this is not "data" but "personal data," the datafied behavior of human beings. It gets pulled out of all that we're doing through the devices we are using such as smartphones, or apps like social networks and messaging tools.

I have this little [fig.4] image here which shows that there are actually four methods of data mining, and I will give examples of that.

One is data-mining by capturing what you're doing in a certain environment. Another method is self-recording, like when you are filling out forms on Facebook. There are two types of data about you. Either tacit information, like your pulse or your body temperature, stuff that you couldn't easily put in words, and then there's information you can verbalize.

Here's an example for capturing: a self-driving car captures data about how you're moving, where you are looking and where you are going. The best example for self-recording is Facebook. This is where you verbalize what you're doing. Here's another example for how to verbalize something: a simple email. There's a lot of words in it, you are expressing something, at the same time an email contains location information, time-stamp, constitutes a relationship between sender and recipient. Your provider, like Gmail, contractually owns this data. Then, as an example for how to capture tacit information: one of those fitness gadgets counting your steps, measuring heart beat, body temperature, and so on.

To sum it up: today we have all the data Cybersyn needed so badly to start functioning. Throughout the last years in my work as a writer I was looking at how, basically, our personal data was

The 4 Methods of Data-Mining

Verbalized

Capture ←——————→ **Self-Recording**

Tacit

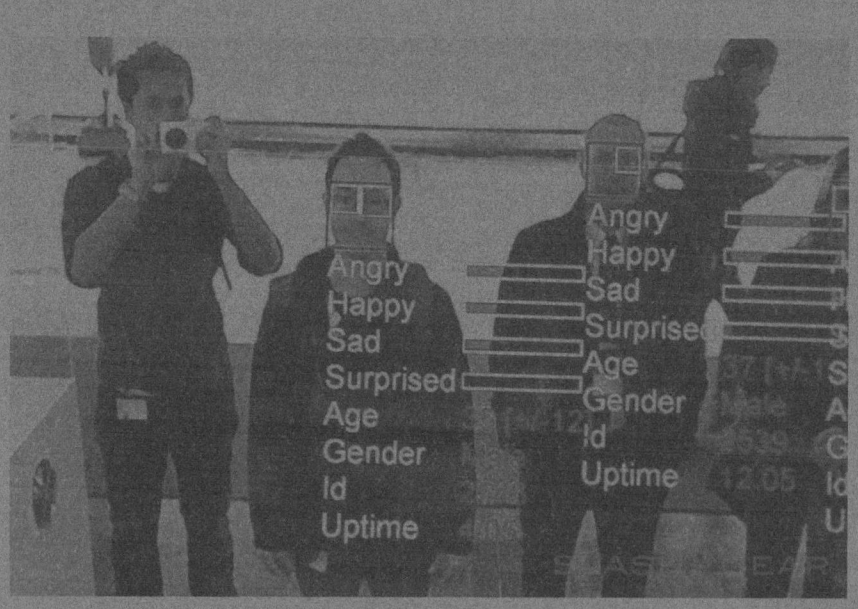

getting captured and marketed. We hand it over to companies by signing all of these contracts, clicking on "yes" to agree to the terms and conditions of any app or a program we want to use.

Let me give you examples. Here's a company capturing our business relationships: LinkedIn. Or an emoji tracker, simply counting and ranking the use of emojis in a given context. Have you ever wondered why you get all these emojis for free on your phone? It's because your moods and sentiments are valuable, marketable information. Imagine you're a weapons trader in some place and you would be able to detect where people feel the most hate. Next example: a book that actually reads you whilst reading. It's called Kindle. All such tools are sensorized: they run statistics on our behavior, and even without us knowing, they capture our user data. Google cooperating with Levi's Jeans. Result: a sensorized pair of jeans. Or in your bathroom. Most of us are probably using these electric toothbrushes, and some of them are probably sending information to a cloud. Just remember when you were a kid, the first thing a doctor would do is look into your mouth, because this is really valuable information about your health condition. Then we have the upcoming Amazon Echo gadget. It's a cloud connected artificial intelligence, a sort of Siri in a box. It's basically a spying tool listening to everything you're saying. Again, it's just capturing your data.

Even if you're not actively equipped with any sort of tool, our environments—here's an example [fig.5] from a supermarket experiment where they are recording how we're behaving and moving within a shop. That way they can figure out what your preferences are. What would be the maximum price you'd pay for a liter of milk in a given situation?

Our entire environment is getting more and more sensorized. They call it smart. The reason is that sensors are becoming cheaper, because they are mass-produced for the billions of smartphones which each contain dozens of them. Today it's sometimes even cheaper to sensorize everything than to not use sensorized parts.

So if you don't want to share your data, and want to get rid of everything, say "go to Africa or India." In come the balloons and drones that Google and Facebook are sending to cover regions that are still off the grid, with the example of the Facebook drones.

The next example, of how you connect your personal biological information with the info you put on the web, is a company called 23andMe. You can send in a little bit of your spit or hair and they will analyze where you're from, what kind of disease you might suffer from in the future. The service is comparatively cheap, like $100 as opposed to the usual price-tag of over $1,500. The results, it turns out after some tests, are very unreliable, but on the other hand 23andMe now has your genetic code information. The founder of that company is Anne Wojcicki, who once was married to Google founder Sergey Brin. Accordingly, Google was one of the first investors to 23andMe. These investors have their hands on your bio-data. It's easy to correlate this with your search data, for example. The whole Silicon Valley gold rush is basically about getting your personal data. It's a big race to get more and more data, individual data, and how to best connect biometric information with user data.

Lastly: you don't own that data. You have signed it away, and you can't control it, because it's in the cloud. You don't have your data on your computer. It's somewhere in the cloud – and what really happens on the other side is ... It's 2014. I'm based in Switzerland where we're hosting the annual World Economic Forum. Already then the big topic was personal data, the "emergence of a new assets class." It's an asset because it's being traded between those companies that own your data.

Here's what the personal data market looks like. [fig.6] You see companies that are like Facebook, sending data and receiving personal data. You see companies like Acxiom – these are called Data Brokers. These companies compile all your data out there and create an identity of you, and offer it for sale. It's a B2B, a business-to-business service for personal data exchange.

This was the sort of research I was doing a couple of years ago, the background for what we'll talking about next.

As a writer and investigative journalist I was always wondering what the risk might be in this, what evil might come out of these data markets. So I made an experiment. In early 2016 I called one of these data brokers and told them I was a Berlin-based start-up planning to sell religious cookbooks in the US. I said I wanted to buy the data of about three to nine million American women. Potential customers, I said. I asked them, if I could get the

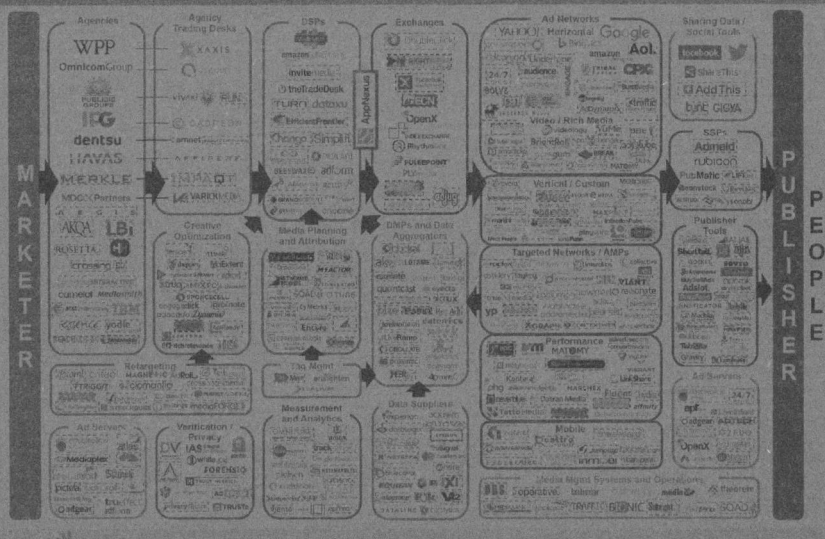

real names and addresses of so many women. They said sure. I said, you know, we are about cookbooks, so could I get more info about what these women buy, what they eat or if they have allergies and all that stuff? The company said no problem, we have all their shopping data, and bonus card infos and memberships. They offered the Facebook accounts, emails, and phone numbers of the women too, in case I wanted to get back to them and ask them if they liked the products. It's that feedback thing. Then I said, you know, my company is into religious cookbooks. Our board is concerned we might hurt our customer's feelings by sending out the wrong cookbook to the wrong person. Could you sort these women into religious categories like Jewish or Christian or Muslim? And then the guy—he was called Bruce—was like "Let me quickly double check," and then "yes we can do that." So if anyone in the US is debating whether there are Muslim registries, there are. There are Jewish registries too, and you can easily buy them. Anyone could. Guess what the price tag was for all that personal data? Three cents per unit, meaning three million persons, from full names to allergies to religion and shopping preference: $90,000. Imagine how great this would be for terrorists. How easily they could target you.

In June 2016 I became interested in a company which at the time had announced they would be working for the Leave EU campaign as digital marketers. The company was called Cambridge Analytica. At the time nobody was really interested in them, they were just one of these companies helping campaigners. But I was really interested because they said they were using personal data to profile individuals. In further researching I stumbled across a story in the *Guardian* where the company was actually mentioned in a case of somebody illegally collecting, or potentially illegally collecting, American voter data through Facebook from unwitting users.

I figured that there was a scientist who had somehow worked on similar methods, so I called him up and we met when he was in Zurich—his name is Michal Kosinski. He was a Cambridge PhD at the time, and told me about the research he was doing. At the Psychometrics Centre at Cambridge University, a group of young researchers were working on a massive personal data analytics project called the MyPersonality project, where Kosinski and his colleague David Stillwell were trying to measure personality just from publicly available personal data. The sort of data each of us is putting out there every day.

Psychometrics is the measuring branch of psychology, the branch where you assign numerical values to different aspects of personalities. It's been around for over one hundred years, but the MyPersonality team simply figured out that one of the most effective resources to measure personality traits is Facebook likes. They built one of these tests that are everywhere on Facebook today, where you click through five questions to find out which superhero type you are—more Spiderman or X-Men. You fill it out, it's just five questions and by the way, but in the little contract that you have to click "yes" to beforehand, you might accidentally give away free access to all the stuff you've liked on Facebook. All your likes. This is what the *Guardian* associated Cambridge Analytica with.

The Cambridge University researchers were, at least, being very transparent to their users at the time. They got all data for research purposes only and with explicit consent by the test users. In no time, MyPersonality built the world's biggest research database for personal data. Hundreds of thousands of users tried the quick test and thus granted access to their likes. This was incredibly valuable. Out of that Kosinski et al. were able to predict personality, just from Facebook likes.

They used the most standard model to do this, which is called the five traits or OCEAN model: Openness, Agreeableness, Extraversion, Conscientiousness, and Neuroticism. Out of these five components you could describe more or less the personality of every person. With 150 Facebook likes they were able to predict better what a person would do in a certain situation—like a model situation: would you turn red, left or right, would you say no or yes to your husband—than a long-time partner or a specific person. With sixty likes they would be better than your closest friends in predicting your personality. And with three hundred likes, they would even be able to predict better than the person herself how she would act in a specific situation. Of course, such analyses can not only be inferred from Facebook likes. Here's an overview paper where the authors analyze how you could actually use other sources of data than Facebook likes, like from the motion-sensor in your phone, such as how abruptly you move your phone. And which places you are going to, if you look at geo-data. This tells a lot about you as a person, and your character.

Cambridge Analytica's MyPersonality describe their project as a sort of machine that produces you out of your digital footprints. Your individual profiles, the big five personality that I mentioned, the psychographics. A men-machine. This was the unique project Kosinski et al. were working on. Kosinski became one of the world's foremost researchers in psychometrics; he's very well respected and a highly-cited scientist. Of course, even back then, he and his colleagues considered how these personalities would actually relate to political opinions. They also experimented: "Could we figure out a person's sexual orientation just from his data traces?," and figured that if you have a combination of liking cosmetics and Lady Gaga as a male, the probability that you're gay is higher.

Then, in early 2014, a colleague approaches Kosinski. Today this colleague is called Dr. Spectre, he actually changed his name to that. Spectre was one of the guys overseeing Kosinski's PhD, and told Kosinski, when he approached him, that there was a company that was really interested in cooperating with MyPersonality, a British company called Strategic Communications Laboratories. They wanted to use the Facebook data sets and the algorithms of the prediction machines that Kosinski had developed. Kosinski was really interested in getting money for his research, but on the other hand he was a bit scared, and it sounded like a lot of money—so he looked up the company and it looked like they were doing something really strange. On their website they said they were doing behavioral influence planning, globally, and mentioned military projects too. Kosinski thought it might be too risky.

And then something really strange happened at Cambridge University. In short, Dr. Spectre disappeared, then this strange incident happens, where the *Guardian* reveals Dr. Spectre is collecting Facebook data from US citizens. The next thing Kosinski sees is a new company named Cambridge Analytica which says they're using methods strikingly similar to his. And they're using them for the Leave EU campaign. Subsequently Kosinski receives loads of calls from former colleagues who are mad at him, because they think he is supporting Brexit. Which he isn't.

Cambridge Analytica went from supporting Brexit to campaigning in the US. So here we are clearly in a right-wing space, simply right-wing cyberspace. Alexander Nix, the CEO of Cambridge Analytica, gave a now famous speech in the summer of 2016, just after Cambridge Analytica had announced they quit working for Ted Cruz, who was one of their early US clients. Within the Republican party, Ted Cruz lost against Trump. During this speech, Nix discloses that they are now working for Donald Trump, and explains in detail his company's approach. Cambridge Analytica, he claims, could construct any voter's psychological profile out of datasets. And it has "5000 data points" per US voter. Out of this data they built the five traits model for each voter in order to help their clients influence them through personalized targeting with information. This is the cybernetic feedback loop: send and receive information and adjust the system. Of course Nix shows the signature Cambridge Analytica control room. In 2016 such a thing of course is a user interface on a computer.

What you see is a map of individuals, which Cambridge Analytica claims to have individually have profiled. The map shows their name, age, and their political position. They claim to buy most of their data from data brokers. You see Acxiom in screenshots of Alexander Nix's presentations, and you see other brand names including the Facebook logo.

Once the company has the data, voter identities are being created algorithmically. Many companies today are doing such things. Cambridge Analytica claims it is different from its competitors because it uses personality rather than demographics to understand voters. Demographics is about your income, age, where you live, how you've been voting in the years before. But personality is really about whether you're a nervous person or not and all of these specific traits.

Nix also explains in this ten minute video how they are actually identifying people by their real names, even though most data is technically anonymous. In the US you can buy voter lists and connect the name on the voter list to other data sets that might have a certain overlap. It becomes clear from the video that Cambridge Analytica was really applying Kosinski's methods. Still, when researching Cambridge Analytica we figured they're also using other methods, so here's one paper where they're talking about how they assess the overall education and intelligence of potential voters in order to influence them.

The next thing is Cambridge Analytica announced that they would be working for Trump. That was during the last four months of his campaign. During their time with Ted Cruz they had already gathered a lot of voter data and built voter models. Now they would target those voters, with the idea to frame your message according to each individual's personality. This is called micro-targeting.

So for example, to convince a neurotic person to support the right to own a gun, the company would suggest an advert that creates a scary situation, like a burglar breaking into an apartment. A weapon thus stands for security. For a more traditionally oriented, less fearful but more agreeable personality—remember the trait "Agreeable"—they would target them with information framing gun ownership as something that comes as a long-standing American tradition. The ad would show father and son, hunting ducks. That's attractive to someone whose profile displays such traits.

This means that if you want to micro-target, if you want to really create individualized feedback loops with every voter, you must make one advertisement per person. How the heck would they do it? This is beyond Kosinski's work, which only is about analyzing individual's data.

I called Nix right after seeing this video—I had him on the phone and lucky me I recorded the conversation—he mentioned they were doing it through Facebook, mostly. This turns out to be not fully true. They delivered more or less the algorithm of how to target the individuals. They joined, at this stage in the campaign, the Republican National Convention Data Team, which actually did nothing very special. They just created ads and sent them through Facebook to individuals they had identified based on the psychographic profiles they had. If you go to Facebook now, everyone can do ad-targeting. Their targeting tool is just how you do advertising on Facebook. Facebook offers thousands of very detailed categories of human beings. They even used to offer "jew-haters." Also, at the time you could even do stuff that related to the color of your skin. If you apply this and add timing and place, you can be very granular. You can target specific persons in a certain situation. You can basically select whom you want to reach out to, and do crazy things. You can send a shocking piece of news to a group of friends just before they meet for dinner. This stuff shows up in your Facebook feeds—that's the targeted information.

Old information, the old style of advertisements, is based on your search queries, on some ideas people might have about you once they see you're a student or something. The Cambridge Analytica style of advertisement is more oriented toward your feelings, because we have to understand that social networks are not networks for information exchange, they are emotional networks. You have "friends" on Facebook, and you "like" stuff. Facebook and Twitter are basically emotional networks. Sending out emotional information is far more effective than other kinds of information. That's why I find the argument quite convincing to have a campaign based on emotions and personality. Trump, and all right-wing haters which are not too shocking, are clearly more suitable candidates for social-media amplification.

Lastly, once a campaign has sent out their ads, they can see how people react to it. How they click on ads, how much time they spent watching it, if they share it etc. So, like in the example of the thermostat, you can measure the room temperature, i.e. How the environment reacts to your stimulus. And then you can adjust your ads. Does a blue background work better than a red one with neurotic types? You can start making test groups. This is called A/B testing. You can vary so many factors. Some of this is manual labor, some is already automated.

This is the sort of real-time feedback mechanism Salvador Allende's teams were dreaming of. First, you gather the information about the persons through all these technical devices, you get the data together, let your algorithms run over it, send info, analyze the feedback, and so on.

During the election we experienced the emergence of a huge right-wing digital space, filled with conspiracy videos, shitstorms, fake-news, dark-ads only visible to some. Surprise, what turns out, Trump wins.

So there's been a lot of debate about whether our report, that we later wrote, was putting too much of an emphasis on how powerful Cambridge Analytica is. I think we are now in the Model T era for individualized or personalized cybernetics. This is very early. We will see much more of this in the future. For me such possibilities give a new meaning to virtual reality. I cannot judge whether this was the decisive tool of the Trump campaign, but Cambridge Analytica, being marketing guys, immediately congratulated President-Elect Donald Trump for the win, and wrote: "It demonstrates the huge impact of our cutting edge data science and we are thrilled to have played such an integral part in President Donald Trump's extraordinary win." As for me: I called Facebook to ask them about the campaign data. They are the best- and only source to see what Cambridge Analytica did and how big their impact was. But Facebook didn't want to help me.

Facebook can basically see everything, how people clicked on ads. Alexander Nix, when I talked to him on the phone, mentioned that actually the Trump campaign was making money off campaigning—had made a profit off the election campaign because they had, through crowdfunding, made so much money using these technologies. Facebook could tell.

I've been looking at today's cybernetic systems for years and had never imagined they would be used for the American elections. But it's so obvious. Again, the story I wrote, which my colleague Mikael Krogerus edited and the researcher Paul-Olivier Dehaye helped gather information for, was from my perspective an illustration of what you can do with personal data today.

This sort of right-wing space is a fully commercialized space. It's right-wing, because right-wing people bought such services. Cambridge Analytica claims to be neutral. It's their customer's political ambitions that count. It turns out that actually the biggest customer they had is a right-wing billionaire named Robert Mercer, one of the most influential, behind-the-scenes figures in contemporary American politics. He also helped during the Brexit Campaign by financing the company and even reportedly co-owning Cambridge Analytica USA.

Now, during the recent Russian phobia thing, the name Cambridge Analytica popped up again because they had to hand over all their mails to Robert Mueller of the FBI who is investigating

Donald Trump's possible Russian connections. There are several legal processes going on against the company in the UK and the US.

It might be the case that some interesting things will come out in the near future, but it's very hard to say.

What I find the most interesting is that this new way of influencing people, of managing society, will not stop after the elections. It will become a standard tool of governance. If I think of virtual reality in the future, and then I think of the government that distributes personalized information to each citizen. Information that would make him believe that, you know, his government is really doing a great job. The infrastructure is all set up for this. There are companies willing to do it, we have seen test-runs and we see people willing to pay for it. Cambridge Analytica worked in Kenya, Australia, and Mexico after our story came out. That's the kind of right-wing space that I have discovered.

> A follow-up note from Hannes Grassegger
> Zurich, February 2018
>
> Think of the Cambridge Analytica story as kind of soft power invasion of your daily routines, a new form of gentle pervasiveness where I am trying to enhance your life with a reality thriller. Something that haunts you once you touch your smartphone or use Tinder. My editor and I, Mikael Krogerus, plus our genius mathematician researcher, formed a narrative from what we saw was just around us. It's now a living, breathing reality, something you can't avoid watching, full of wonderful and amazing and wicked characters that lead a real life full of real secrets they know about each other, and also about us—and they are revealing them slowly but surely. Soon maybe the dragons will come in. And whilst you are watching it, seeing posh Etonian Alexander Nix and pink-haired Christopher Wylie the whistleblower you are starting to understand you yourself need to change your life, because if not you will be drawn into that world you thought you was just a dark spectacle. It is not. It is digital business. Nothing but that. And actually you are already a part of it. Mostly everyone is. Trump is as true as Zuckerberg.

Markus Miessen (MM)   Thank you so much, Hannes! First question: of course this presents quite a gloomy outlook, but is there any way to somehow, even on a personal level, withdraw from this?

HG   As I said, once our environments are sensorized, you're not able to withhold data anymore. And if you can draw information about your personality from all sorts of things like how you move your face, I don't think there's any way back. After the report, Twitter—they were very concerned that their company had become sort of a weapon—asked me, "What would be the silver bullet to solve, we don't want to be a weapon." I said the only thing I could imagine is total transparency for third parties to see what is happening on your platform.

      I'd say to Facebook: give me the information of what the Russians sent out to whom, who bought it, what the Trump campaign said about it. At least then we can see then what's going on.[1] I wrote a little book four years ago, which argues, from the bottom of my economist's heart, that I think we should own our data. I should have ownership of it, meaning I should be able to decide who gets my personal data and who doesn't. And I should be compensated for that. That might be an economist's answer, and there might be many problems associated with that, but it's what I'm thinking.

MM   Technically, do you think this may be possible?

HG   No. But because technically this is not possible, we need a rights-based approach. What we are in now reminds me of a feudal system, of medieval times where the overlords own the fruit of your land, and they decide when to kill you and lock you in. Now people are asking me what kind of helmet they should get. I would suggest not a helmet but a redistribution of ownership, like back when we introduced contracts between the landowners and the farmers. Like today when you give employees rights over their product.

      There is a giant opportunity just waiting for all of us if we introduce data ownership. But I fear the opposite will happen. Historically, we've been raised in a time when everything was open. But if you look at history—"Gote-borg"—comes from the word for castle in Swedish. There are walls associated with this city and its fortresses. At worst, we had this brief period where we didn't have walls, where we had liberal environments protected by law, but now, to me, it looks like data ownership will not win. People will use firewalls, and encryption and attacks and so on. Walls will be built.

Question One   In the early days of tech, designers were part of data mining, even Charles and Ray Eames designed and formed new technology. What do you think of the role of designers today?

HG   I think designers are currently helpful in making people more addicted to these data collection machines. These are great, well-paid jobs for designers. I don't see anyone–thus far–paying designers in ordinary life for helping us out of this situation.

But it might be a market opportunity to create a mechanism that eases this situation a bit. Right now I do think all talking about revolutionary design is just fancy talking. Most people are actually figuring out the right color set and the right frame to make you spend more time on each of these platforms.

Question Two   There are also devices designed to help you hide, and hide your information, on the Internet.

HG   This is armor too, from my perspective. This is stealth mode. I think actually what we need is kind of not a technical solution to this, since this is a social, political, and economic issue. I think what is really helpful is the debate amongst designers. Economists don't have such debates like you guys are having. More debate amongst designers is already a very useful thing. Ultimately it informs politics. I read a lot of design and arts news, then I write a report in our magazine, and it ends up in a politician's hand or entrepreneur's hands, and that's one way that design can inform.

Christina Varvia (CV)   How about legislation? To tamper with the election would, in principle, be illegal, correct? If you have a company that claims they've done just that, then what is the impact? Are they able to assess whether it was done or not, because technologically they couldn't even know what it does?

HG   I tried to figure this out, during the research, because it's a brilliant question—as equally yours is, really. I called a couple leading data protection authorities on the EU level, in academia. They were not able to answer it clearly. I had just one simple question: Does data law in the UK fall under European law? Under European law you're not allowed to do political profiling based on personal data without explicitly asking each person, whether I can create such a profile. Of five leading authorities, none had a definitive answer. They would say the answer would be in general terms yes—but there might be ways that local legislation allows for certain loopholes, which I don't know yet, which is what these companies are actively using.

That's the way things are done in times of the gold rush. Uber is just extending its network and then waiting for the first lawsuits to come in. Political companies are very much doing the same. Because everyone in the legal sphere is like "That sounds so technical, I don't know this new technology thing." This is a human factor that is just playing out, and will continue for a while I think. So I don't believe in the German answer, meaning extending the legal laws of the government overseeing this. I don't think it will really work, because this is far too useful for the government, I don't even see their self-interest in that. Politics can build and maintain power just with those same tools.

MM   So, in terms of the market, say if I wanted to work with Cambridge Analytica …

HG   You would call them.

MM   Would it be a first come, first served situation?

HG   Yes. After I wrote the article, the head of the company that my little brother—a very nice guy who likes my reports and so shares them—came back and said: "This sounds really interesting, what Cambridge Analytica does." The next month they invited them to speak.

So, they do. Alexander Nix walks right in front of my little brother, of course he didn't know it in that situation who my little brother was. Everyone in the company was scared of my little brother speaking out, so they shielded him away, but he managed to slip into the elevator with Alexander Nix. The two men were in the elevator. My brother says, "Hey you're Alexander Nix, right?" and Alexander Nix says, "Of course." Nix is very British. So he says, "My name is Vincent Grassegger, I'm the brother of Hannes Grassegger, who wrote the report about your company." Nix had been working on elections in revolutionary settings, developing countries, like really bad stuff. So he pulls out his business card, gave it to my little brother and says, "Um. Tell him he should call me."

       They're having great business right now, but they're also facing severe legal challenges, because in the UK there's a lot of legal investigations.[2] It's probably illegal what they did, but soon judges will decide, because Cambridge Analytica is suing my colleague at the *Guardian*, who is continuing to write about all of this. It's strangely enough the same lawyers Putin is using.

Question Three   I was wondering to what degree is it possible to see how these tools actually make people change their mind. I'm thinking of how media, even before the digital, shows that most people are just interested in affirming beliefs, they buy the newspaper they like.

HG   This is a very good question, a core question again. During the 1950s there was this debate about "deep psychology" and how supermarkets would be able to manipulate all the consumers by arranging the color sets, and a lot of people would be shopping for things they wouldn't need. Then in the late '60s and '70s you had the debate about brainwashing and people getting totally manipulated, returning to the United States after wars and becoming terrorists and sleepers on call—there are great movies about this—and now we have a recurring theme, the manipulation and brainwashing thing.

       I would rather stick with what is said about affirming, and so what we saw when Nix was presenting these two advertisements is that you put a person like you, probably who's totally not interested in supporting guns, you know, and frame the message in a way that you would agree. Make you affirm something. This is not really manipulating you, this is not brainwashing but framing a certain thing in a way that you would be OK with. And then it's about activating you. I don't believe in brainwashing, but there's this study which a colleague of Kosinski's, Sandra Matz, did where they presented people with two ads on Facebook, framed according to their psychological profile. One would be the opposite of what they figured your type is and one would totally go with your type. And they compare how people clicked on each ad. They figured people are really much more likely to click on an ad which suits the type of personality that they identified. There's a potential that this stuff really works, and if you think about how many people are currently using Facebook advertisements, Facebook ad targeting, then it's a major market. I don't think companies pay billions for it just for fun. These people believe it works for them. And of course as a Facebook customer, you get feedback numbers. Robert Mercer invested in Cambridge Analytica, and actually founded one of the world's most sophisticated artificial intelligence investment funds himself, so he knows the matter quite well. I think he wouldn't invest in a scam, being a renowned software developer himself.

    Finally, there is the whole question of information warfare. This is basically the field that Strategic Communication Laboratories is based in, so they do different information operations and psychological operations, so-called psy-ops. Russia is doing similar stuff, and here in Sweden you have a commission working with your government to detect such stuff. We can certainly discuss this later.

Rechte Räume
Stephan Trüby

Thank you very much, Hannes. Hello everyone, I am very glad to be here—my name is Stephan Trüby.

I was thinking about how architecture comes into the picture. I have the intuition that what I will be talking about could be the worst possible end of the story that Hannes told, so it's not a happy end. It's an end that we, probably—if you allow me the "we" for a moment—have to avoid at all costs.

      It's obviously not that easy to link architecture, as individual buildings, to political positions, as it is extremely difficult to link habits or gestures to political ideology. What I would like to start with is to look at architecture in a very basic way. We could describe it as the how the Antifa[3] would look at architecture. The Antifa isn't really interested in symbols or in architectural qualities, and the Antifa is definitely not interested in proportions and things like that. The Antifa is basically interested in three things about places: 1—addresses, 2—boundaries and boundary conditions, and 3—colors. Maybe Antifa could be described as the Stone Age version of Cambridge Analytica. They collect address data of right-wing extremists.

      I should mention at this point that in the context of my topic I'm not a big fan of the term populism. In this case of extremism, far-right extremism—you could look at Trump, but also the AfD[4]—the boundaries between populism and extremism are extremely fluid. One moves into the other. Populism is probably the wrong term for what I will describe now.

      I collected research about right-wing spaces, between three and four hundred addresses of buildings, people, and institutions

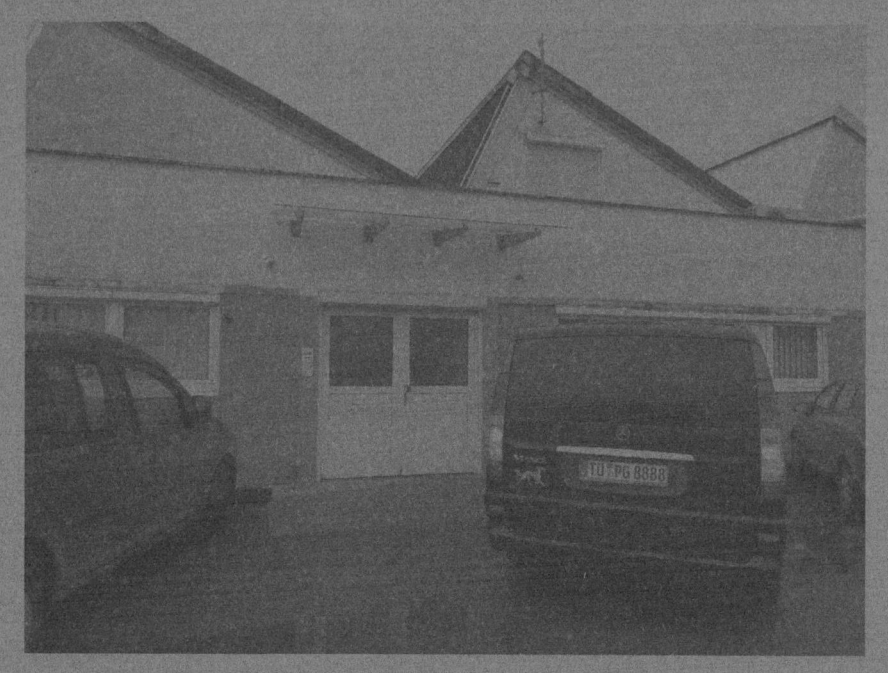

not only in Germany but also in Europe and in the US. In a manner similar to how the Antifa are doing it, I started to travel to many of these places. I tried to link my family holidays with the highest density of addresses I could come across. The whole trip started close to my hometown in Stuttgart, in a student town called Tübingen. Maybe some of you have heard of it. Tübingen is a rather leftist city governed by a green mayor. But the city and its region are also the center of the two most important right-wing publishing houses in Germany and in the German speaking part of the world. One is called Grabert Verlag, and the other, based in Rottenburg near Tübingen, is called Kopp Verlag. Wigbert Grabert, the owner of Grabert Verlag, is basically a neo-Nazi and lives in a slightly modest house. There's nothing interesting to say about its architecture except that it looks a bit neurotic, slightly paranoid with its many cameras, but the people who live here do indeed get attacked sometimes by Antifa. On the façade of this building you can find many traces of colors from the color bombs the Antifa throw.

  Let's start with addresses. When I started to work on this list and also to work on the journey, I initially became obsessed with numbers. Maybe I'm talking about accidents, but the fact that so many 18's appear in this list—the "18" is a German code for A-H, Adolf Hitler—is not an accident anymore. For example, Wigbert Grabert's house in Tübingen has the address Am Apfelberg 18, and many more neo-Nazi homes in Germany live in a number "18." I also found hidden number codes at the neo-Nazi Hohenrain Versandhaus in Tübingen, owned by Bernhard Grabert, the son of Wigbert. When I arrived there, a car with the car plate code 8888 stood in front of the entrance [Fig. 7]. This stands for "Heil Hitler, Heil Hitler." These are not accidents, this is obviously highly planned.

  Secondly: boundary conditions. In Germany there's a neo-Nazi singer-songwriter who's also part of the NPD named Frank Rennicke. He bought a former school building in Feilitzsch close to Hof, Frankonia, and turned it into kind of a camp for his family and his closest friends. We see from his house he's very interested in keeping boundaries—but also in flags. When I went there on the 20th of April, which is Hitler's birthday, there was a party going on.

The third thing I was talking about (first numbers, then boundary conditions) is color. Colors appear in the facade, including of Wigbert Graberts's house, as traces of protest. If you visit right-wing spaces, you either see the traces of color bombs or they are newly painted and redone frequently, so there's often fresh color on these buildings.

The big question now is what to do with this list? There's also a moral question behind it. Do we invite, with our research, violence in the form of people getting injured or even killed by attacks etc.? We haven't reached a conclusion yet.

Of course, we also need to talk about the relationship between stone and flesh, about substance, and about architecture as built matter and ideology. I'm coming from Munich and I'm teaching in Munich, where at the moment there's an interesting debate which has to do with the infamous Haus der Kunst building, the first big public Nazi architecture. It was built from 1933 to 1937 by Paul Ludwig Troost. Currently, it looks like this: a row of trees hide the residue of Nazism in the cityscape. The building needs a renovation, and David Chipperfield Architects has been commissioned to do it. One of the architect's intentions is to get rid of the trees, which has led to a highly politicized debate. People like Chipperfield say Germans are done with Nazism. We can keep the stone and get rid of the trees, there's no new Hitler rising. Be relaxed about it, that's his argument. Others are less sure.

At the same time, another debate unfolded around Hitler's birth house in Braunau am Inn, Austria, about 100 kilometers away from Munich [Fig. 8]. Obviously Adolf Hitler wasn't born here as a Nazi, he became a Nazi in Munich afterwards. But here the political debate in Austria goes in the direction of erasing the whole building because the stone, which, some people say, is not immune. Here, the little baby Adolf—definitely not a Nazi at all—turned this building into something really evil that quite a few people want to get rid of. The comparison between how people deal with Hitler's birth house in Braunau, a house neither built nor inhabited by Nazis, and the Haus der Kunst, a building definitely built by Nazis, shows us the difficulty of linking buildings to political positions like Left or Right.

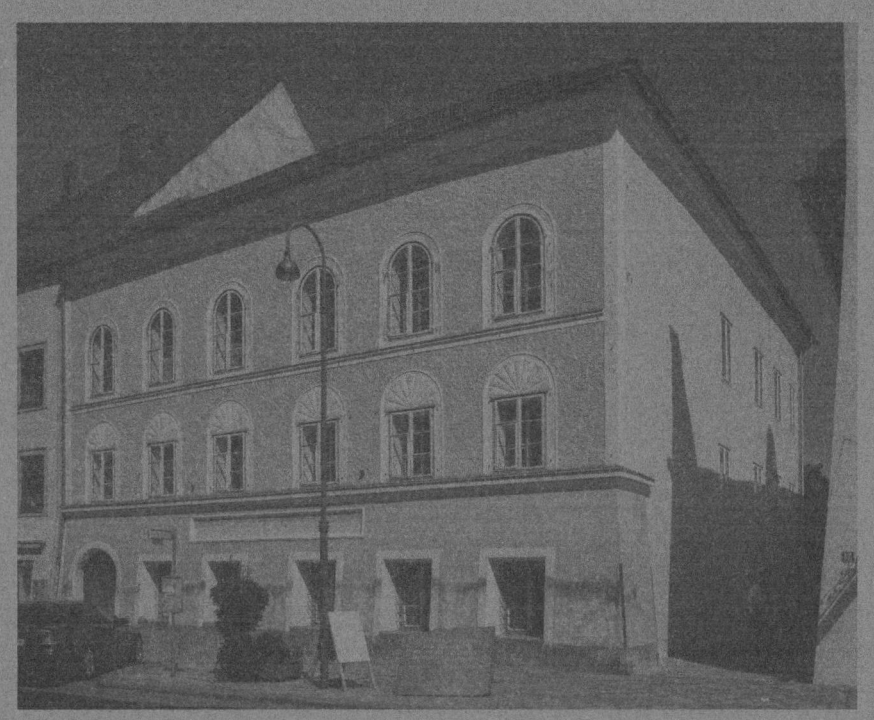

The more I think about this, the more I am convinced of a need to "double up" our understanding of left versus right. In a recent article in the book *The Great Regression* (2017), Slavoj Žižek wrote that there's always a double version of the political Right and a double version of the political Left. Within the Left we can distinguish a universalist Left and an anti-globalist Left, and some of these anti-globalists are also anti-semitic. Similarly, within the Right, we can distinguish a neoliberal and sometimes even libertarian Right linked to global capitalism, and there's also a kind of anticapitalist Right—called *völkisch* Right in German—a patriotic nationalist Right and anti-semitic Right. Žižek writes that the axis between the two Rights is perfectly represented by Donald Trump, and the political situations in India or Russia.

I turned Žižek's words into a diagram and extended it with two additional links between the leftist and the rightist spectrum [Fig. 9], which could be called "Progressive Liberalism" on the one hand—Angela Merkel or Hillary Clinton could be positioned somewhere on this link—and "Querfront" or "Third Position" on the other. The latter notion can explain some of the spectacular careers of activists and intellectuals especially in Germany, who, in the late sixties, started as communists and turned later into right-wing nationalists like Horst Mahler and others.

We can also position architects within the diagram. Rem Koolhaas, for example, is definitely "at home" in the upper part of the diagram, for those who know him more on the leftist side. Not surprisingly he is a fan of generic architecture, a global architecture that doesn't allude to local buildings. Very often this kind of architecture gets supported by right-wing libertarians as well as by leftist universalists. The countermovement against this kind of architecture comes also from both the Left and the Right and currently maybe often more aggressively from the Right: there are Facebook pages like "Architectural Revival" which is a British page led by Rob and Léon Krier fans. They go against globalist architecture and believe in something like national identity. They want to re-establish beauty in architecture. And if we go to the Facebook pages of the Identitarian Movement in Germany or Switzerland for example, you find comments on architecture that could have been drawn by Léon Krier thirty or forty years ago.

November 25, 2017

They are pretty successful in turning a formerly emancipatory notion like "identity" into something latently or openly racist.

Amongst architects who've written prominently, the only person who could be positioned in the top right part of the diagram, in the right-wing-libertarian corner, is Patrik Schumacher.

MM   For those of you who aren't coming from the architecture field, Patrik Schumacher was second in command at Zaha Hadid's office, and now basically runs Zaha Hadid Architects.

ST   And just to add a couple more names to the diagram: Léon Krier is definitely to be positioned in the lower part of the diagram, most likely leaning toward the right. He wrote a book on the architecture of Albert Speer, ignoring his career as a war criminal, and obviously loves it. Imre Makovecz, whose "organic" and expressionist architecture has been favored by the right-wing regime of Viktor Orbán [Fig. 10], can be positioned in the lower left corner. Drawing inspiration from National Romanticism, Makovecz became a fierce nationalist and anti-communist, a fan of Miklós Horthy — Hitler's ally in Hungary — and an anti-Semite. As Eva S. Balogh once made clear, Makovecz repeatedly talked disparagingly about Jewish leftist liberals like Ágnes Heller and György Konrád. When a reporter once asked Makovecz whether his scathing remarks about "Heller and company" had anything to do with their Jewishness, his answer was: "I can't leave it out, even if I stand on my head. They always have something to criticize the Hungarian nation for; they have a superiority complex; they live with the idea of being the chosen people."

There's also a theory around right-wing positions in architecture, especially in the German speaking context. Three names are especially important in this context: Paul Schultze-Naumburg, Leopold Ziegler and Arthur Moeller van den Bruck. I don't have time to go into the details of their theories now, but one point to make clear, and also important for the Swedish context, is the opposition between romanticism and classicism. In this city, Gothenburg, with buildings by Gunnar Asplund and others, I think we have to keep in mind that even in the 1920s in Germany

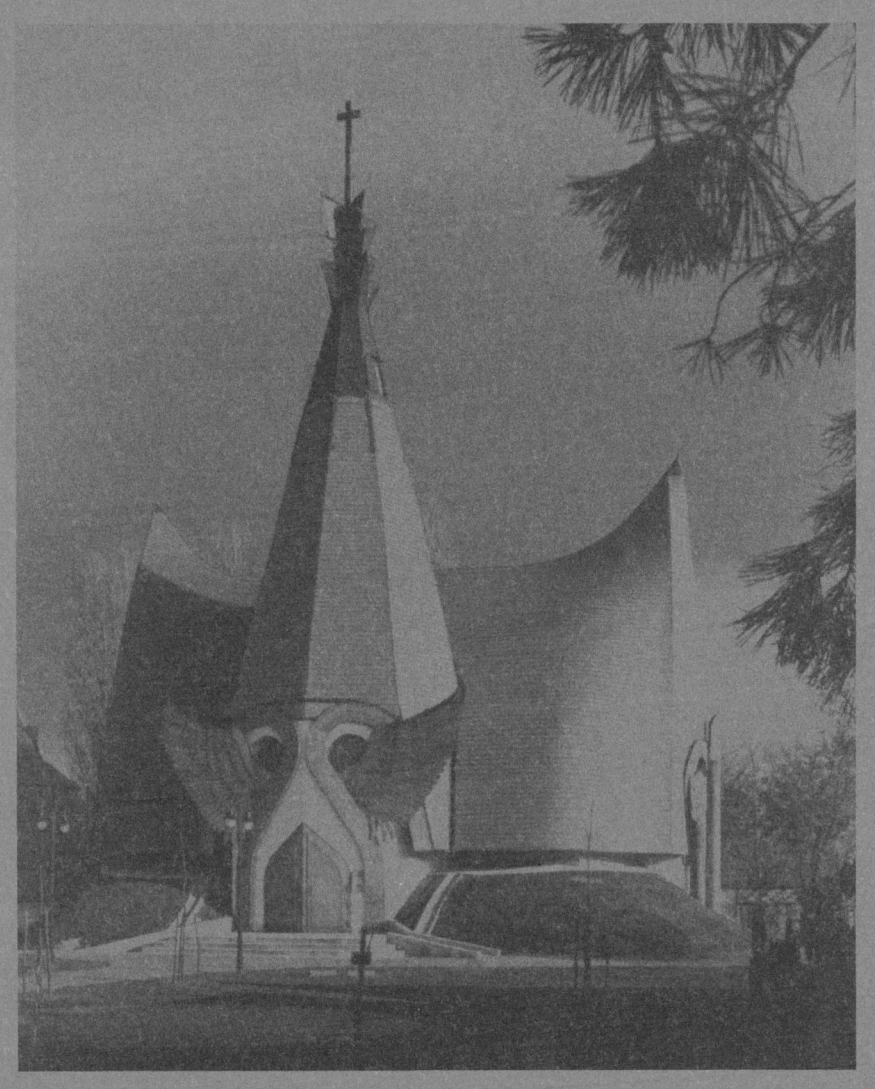

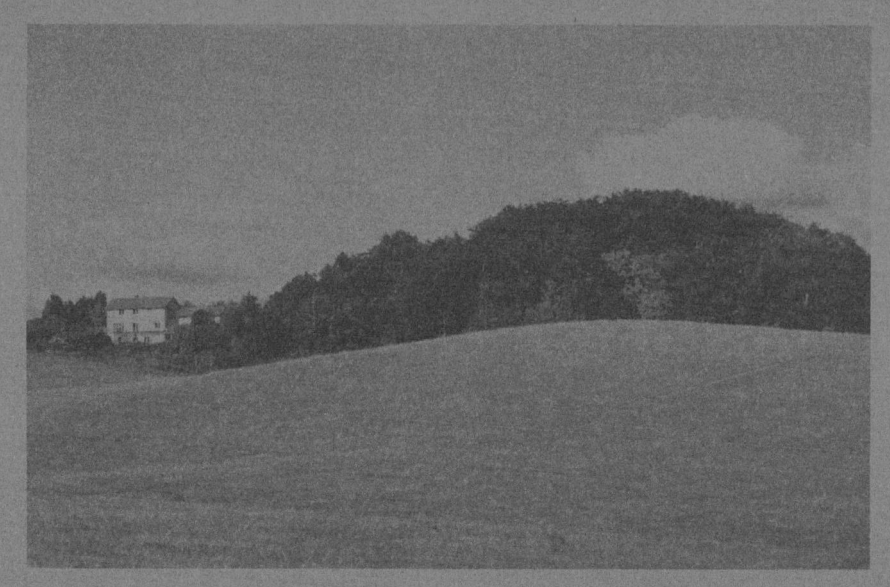

11

there was a big debate between reactionary architects and theorists who either thought that romanticism or classicism was the solution for their problems. Leopold Ziegler, for example, wrote a book called *Die florentinische Introduktion* (1911) in which he despised Renaissance architecture. Ziegler thought that medieval architecture was the triumph, and that we need to go back to that kind of architecture. He was part of the expressionist movement in the 1920s. Moeller van den Bruck was the counterpart to Leopold Ziegler. He hated expressionism, he hated medieval architecture, and wanted to establish a Prussian style of architecture. If you follow the debate in the 1990s and early 2000s in Berlin, suddenly architects like Jürgen Sawade and Hans Kollhoff started to talk again about Prussian architecture, and sometimes referenced, very naively, people like Moeller van den Bruck, who was an anti-semitic reactionary. Let's keep in mind that Ziegler's crystalline architecture and its longing for the medieval, its hatred for the Renaissance, went counter to Moeller van den Bruck's Prussian style and its argument for classicism against Romanticism and the medieval.

I would like to present now a very brief typology of right-wing spaces in the German and international context that I work on, starting with the "lonesome house." In Germany there's a prominent writer called Botho Strauß. He lives in a "lonesome house" in Brandenburg, near Berlin, and wrote a novel called *Die Fehler des Kopiste*n about taking his little son on a walk around the house. In this novel you find a sentence like: "I would rather live in a dying but vital nation"—he uses the term *Volk*—"than in one that is being rejuvenated by being mixed together by foreign people primarily on the basis of economic and demographic speculation." It's a xenophobic and latently neo-fascist statement. If you read the book, you find such highly reactionary positions throughout. He describes himself as the "last German," and his own house as the last German house in the wilderness. That's the house, photographed by the writer Joachim Bessing [Fig. 11]. I would like to compare this residence with another "lonesome house," the one inhabited by Udo Pastörs, a politician of the National Party of Germany (NPD) and one of the key figures of neo-Nazism in Germany. On a site in the Mecklenburg Elbe

Valley Nature Park, which could legally only have been built on if a tree nursery was built as well though it never happened, Pastörs constructed a stately manor with a dead-straight drive lined with German oaks leading seventy yards to the entrance door. The estate lies on a country road with the expressive name *Zum Reizen* (literally, to stimulate or provoke) and was constructed according to a model of a *Wehrhof* (a fortified structure) from the Memel Territory. It was designed and built by the Lüneburg building contractor Manfred Börm, who had several previous convictions for neo-Nazi activities. Pastörs is currently planning a German model village on his estate; he has already had right-wing youths build a red-brick duplex next to the main house, and there's more coming. The whole house is also a frequent stage set for the NPD-channel Deutsche Stimme TV.

  My second typology are "völkisch settlements," communities to counter the death of the Volk in the perspective of their constructors. They have sprung up in the last few years, primarily in rural areas of eastern Germany, but also to a lesser extent in Bavaria, Hessen, Lower Saxony, and Schleswig-Holstein. Filled with disgust at any kind of metropolitan multicultural way of life, many NPD cadres and AfD adherents seek their salvation in the countryside. In Mecklenburg-Vorpommern, far away from people with immigrant backgrounds, imagined or real, right-wing settlers have a special fondness for rehearsing the "preservation of the German Volk" in extremely low-priced real estate. Initially in the guise of friendly neighbors, they infiltrate clubs, kindergartens, and schools. Close to Pastör's house, in Klaber, in the hilly area of Mecklenburg, the attempts of the neo-right to grab land are particularly evident. In a concerted campaign, a stonemason, an artist blacksmith, a bookbinder, a midwife, and many others on the extreme right moved into some empty houses and gradually took over almost all aspects of village life. Political scientist and investigator of right-wing extremism Andrea Röpke has also recognized all too familiar anti-Semitic statements in the rustic, craft orientation of the group, who describe themselves as "creatively" perceptive doers, and seek to differentiate themselves from the image of "money-grubbing, international Jewish financial capital." The same strategy was also applied by in Scandinavia during the

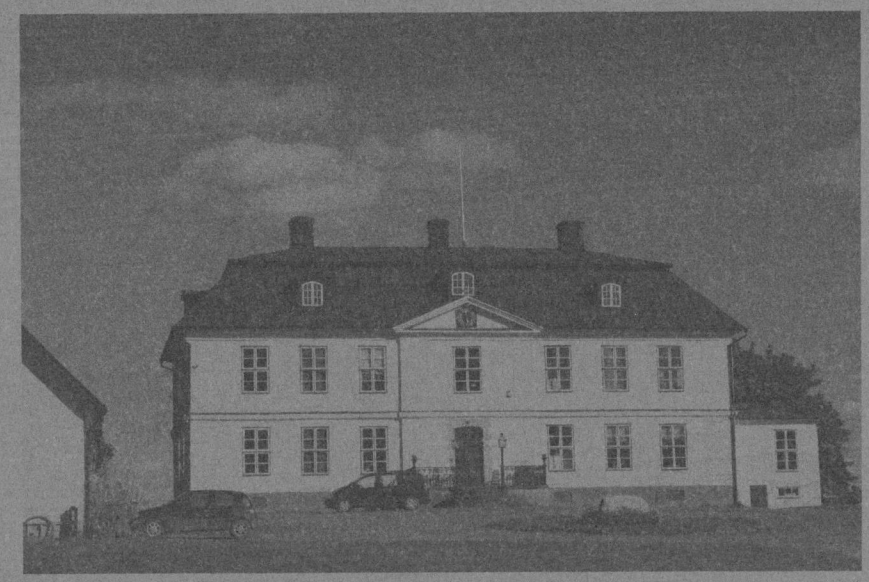

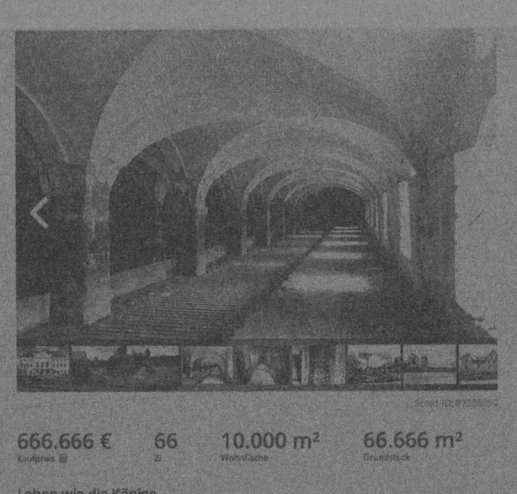

1990s, when Sweden was the refuge of German Nazis like Jürgen Rieger, who hoped to find there a fertile ground for their (Nordic) ideas. In 1995, Rieger bought the estate Sveneby Säteri close to Mariestad, including 650 hectares of land [Fig. 12]. With advertisements, he tried to attract racist Germans and Swedes to settle on his lands, amongst them Klas Lund, who bought another estate there close to Sveneby Säteri. By the way, it seems that nowadays the direction has reversed: In 2007, the Swedish right-wing extremist Patrik Brinkmann moved to Berlin. He bought a villa in Zehlendorf, where he tried to establish a think tank of modern-day racism known as "ethnopluralism" in Europe.

The third typology is the völkisch community around castles. Having been inscribed in the collective memory as monumental landmarks spanning centuries (not to mention being compatible with national romantic traditions and ideas of corporative, authoritarian social systems), converted sheds, manor houses, and castles are particularly apt for the purpose of giving right-wing authoritarian societies an adequate backdrop. This can be exemplified with the German neo-Nazi Karl-Heinz Hoffmann, who inhabited many castles including in earlier times together with the paramilitary sports group Wehrsportgruppe Hoffmann, his private army, which at times comprised more than four hundred men. The now seventy-eight-year-old neo-Nazi initially moved into Schloss Almoshof in Nuremburg in 1974, before moving in 1978 to a new location east of Erlangen, Schloss Ermreuth, which had served as a Nazi party Gauführer school in the Third Reich. In 2004, together with his partner Franziska Birkmann, he purchased Schloss Kohren-Sahlis in Saxony, [Fig. 13] an estate first mentioned in official records in 1551 and previously inhabited by the anti-Semitic poet Börries Baron von Münchhausen, who in 1944 had been included by Adolf Hitler in the "God-gifted list of indispensable writers." For the upkeep of the estate, which includes a gatehouse, stables, storehouses, a bowling alley, a still, and a rococo park, mostly dating from the eighteenth century, Hoffmann set up the Schloss Sahlis Fiduciary Cultural Foundation (Fiduziarische Kulturstiftung Schloss Sahlis), where in his role as "curator," Hoffman established an organic farm breeding Mangalica woolly pigs. Hoffmann claims that he is not a Nazi, but rather "a socialist eco-fascist." For his cultural foundation, which was declared a nonprofit organization and populated not only by pigs but also by a right-wing brotherhood, he obtained €130,000 in public funding from the Free State of Saxony. Yet this did not prevent the Schloss being foreclosed upon. The castle was reported as being up for sale, advertised online under the banner "Live like a King," with sixty-six rooms, spread out over a large property comprising 66,666 square meters (sixteen acres), are offered at a price of €666,666. In this context I could also mention Rittergut Schnellroda, the estate owned by the far-right publishers Götz Kubitschek and Ellen Kositza, or Nöbeditz estate, the home owned by André Poggenburg, an AfD politician in Saxony-Anhalt.

The fourth and last example typology I would like to talk about is located in inner cities. Even though the architectural metapolitics of German right-wing populists and extremists primarily takes place in rural areas—in isolated homes, villages, remote manorial estates, castles, and stately homes—it should be noted that rightist spaces are by no means limited to the countryside. The völkisch interventions out in the countryside should be seen as a complement to architectural endeavors located in considerably more urban domains. These protean ventures can all be placed at the intersection of architecture and the culture of remembrance in the service of a new Germany, about which architecture theorist Philipp Oswalt once wrote that it dreamed "not merely of another future but of another past." This "other history" can be traced in reconstructions. Even if the vast majority of reconstruction projects in Germany are supported by a rather broad spectrum of parties, which is to say it is not only right-wing populist and far-right parties that want to reconstruct, it is still noticeable that the architecture pages of Germany's neo-right magazines are almost exclusively devoted to issues of reconstruction. In the xenophobic, youth-oriented magazine *Blaue Narzisse* from Chemnitz, for example, Maximilian Zech advocates for more "beauty and sense of tradition in building design," which he believes can be discerned in the reconstructed Adlon Hotel in Berlin. Even Peter Stephan, one of the most important advocates of reconstruction and professor of architectural history at the Potsdam University of Applied Sciences, seeks to align reconstruction themes with right-wing

14

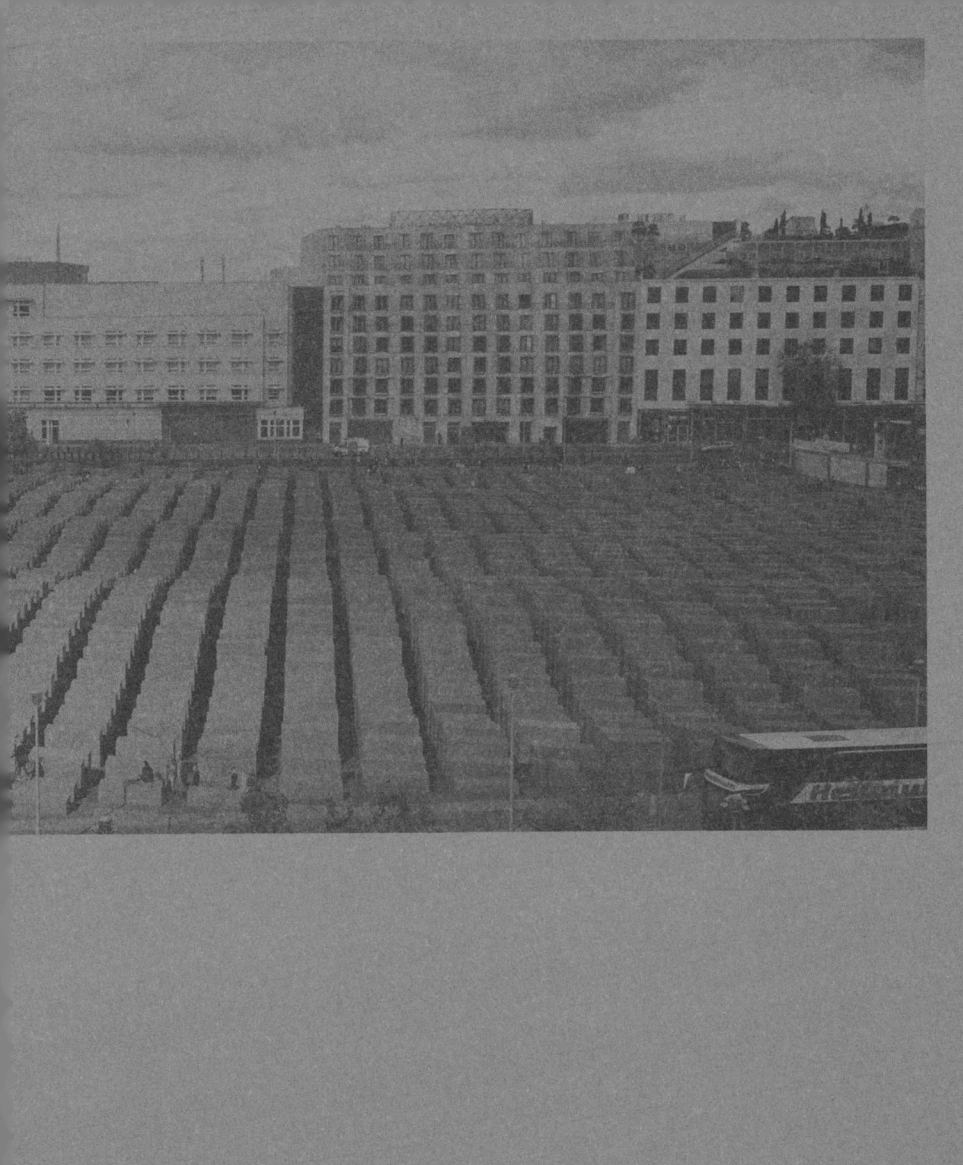

sections of society. For example, with the use of public events and a university research project, he set out to uncouple the history of the Garrison Church in Potsdam, which was demolished in 1968, from what occurred in front of it on March 21, 1933: the so-called Day of Potsdam, when Hitler and President of the Reich Paul von Hindenburg shook hands and thus sealed the disastrous alliance between National Socialist and German national powers.

For many right-wing populists and far-right extremists, the reconstruction of "another" history corresponds with the marginalization of the "one" history. Speaking in an interview with the American station CBN on March 10, 2016, Björn Höcke asserted that "Germans have a one-sided fixation with their dark sides. We have thus developed a culture of guilt that makes it impossible for us to generate a healthy national consciousness, a vibrant patriotism." At the so-called "Kyffhäuser meeting" on June 4, 2016, to which the völkisch nationalistic "wing" of the AfD had sent out invitations, Höcke proclaimed, "A nation that no longer erects monuments but only memorials has no future." What this means in concrete terms is clearly articulated by Höcke's friend Poggenburg when he sputters with monumental degeneracy about the "ugly aesthetics" of Peter Eisenman's Holocaust Memorial in Berlin [Fig. 14] and without showing the slightest restraint, proposes tearing it down. A similar line was taken by the Baden Württemberg parliamentary delegate Wolfgang Gedeon when, speaking on the SWR radio station on June 2, 2016, he stated, "At the heart of the commemorative site there should be something positive. If the [Holocaust Memorial] is somewhere on the periphery ... I have nothing against that."

I would like to finish with small fragments of this panorama beyond Germany. I would like to start with Italy, since this country is interesting for our subject because there we can find the most established "inner city culture" of right-wing spaces anywhere. One movement is particularly relevant for us: Casa Pound, a fascist political party born as political movement arising from the squatting of a state-owned building in the neighborhood of Esquilino in Rome on December 26, 2003. [Fig. 15] The building, named after the American fascist poet Ezra Pound, is located on via Napoleone III. Over the years Casa Pound became part of an

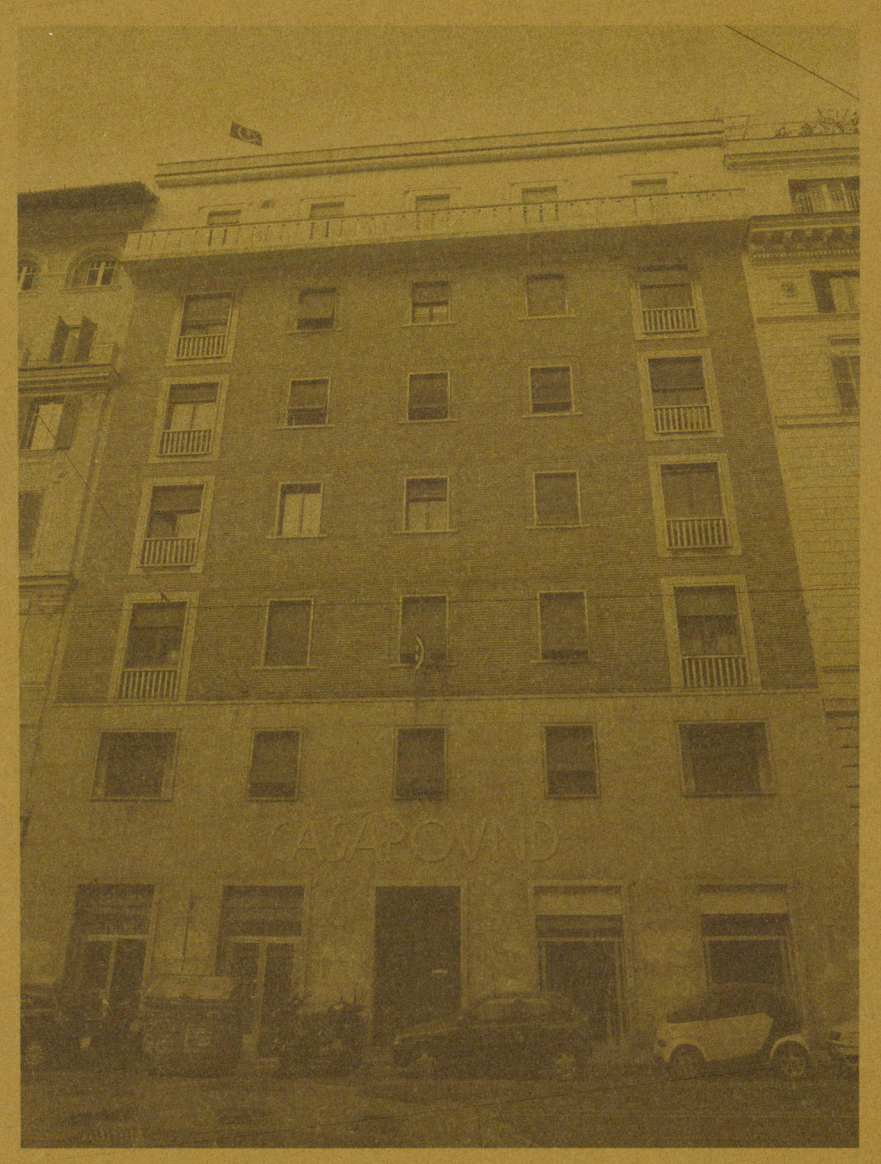

elaborate network of right-wing spaces in Rome, including bars, fashion shops and bookstores. Casa Pound also serves as the blueprint for efforts of the German Identitarian Movement to establish an inner city bridgehead in the city of Halle, at Adam-Kuckhoff-Straße 16. A slight difference in strategy is that in Halle they are not squatting but legally inhabiting a building, one bought by the far-right millionaire from Lower Frankonia Helmut Englmann. Despite the economic difference, the Halle house echoes the Casa Pound's efforts in Rome fifteen years earlier to right-wing politics as lifestyle subculture in the inner city.

France is also interesting in this regard. There, in contrast to Italy, right-wing spaces are primarily located in rural areas. Let's have a look at Les Brigandes for example, the Identarian women's group which performs songs that target Muslims, Jews, journalists, gays, Jesuits, freemasons, politicians and Pope Francis. They live in the small town called Salvetat in the Black Mountains, in a kind of hippie commune of about thirty people. An online petition against the group has gathered nearly 1,500 signatures, more than the population of the town, which has 1,100 residents. Obviously, phenomena like Les Brigandes are unimaginable without the rise of the Front National in France. Ever since the five-kilogram dynamite bomb attack on Jean-Marie Le Pen's Paris apartment at 9 Villa Poirier in 1976, the private living conditions of the Le Pen family has been of public interest. In 1977, Le Pen inherited a fortune from Hubert Lambert (1934–1976), son of the cement industrialist Leon Lambert (1877–1952). Hubert Lambert was a political supporter of Le Pen and provided thirty million francs (approximately five million euros) to Le Pen, as well as his three-storey eleven-room mansion at 8 Parc de Montretout, Saint-Cloud (built by Napoleon III for his chief of staff Jean-François Mocquard). The two daughters of Jean-Marie Le Pen, Yann and Marine—herself the currently most prominent politician of Front National—both live on the grounds of Montretout. Together with his wife, Jean-Marie Le Pen also owns a two-story townhouse on the Rue Hortense in Rueil-Malmaison and another house in his hometown of La Trinité-sur-Mer. My last French example is Renaud Camus, a French writer of both prose fiction and primarily right-wing political polemics, mainly prominent for his book on the Grand Remplacement (the "great replacement" in English), in which he criticizes Muslim immigration from the Middle East and North Africa to France claiming they threaten to "mutate" the country and its culture permanently. He lives in Château de Plieux (South-West France) where he organizes art exhibitions and runs his own political party, the Party of "Non-Nuisance" (Parti de L'In-Nocence), even though he has openly supported Marine Le Pen.

  I could go on, with examples from other countries like Poland, Hungary, Austria, Switzerland, the Netherlands, or the US—in all these countries I collected a huge amount of information regarding right-wing spaces—but for the sake of time I will stop my panorama here.

  I would like to conclude with an art project, one could say, or a political project that happened on this past Monday, less than a week ago, in Germany. I didn't mention the house of Björn Höcke, one of the far-right politicians in Germany. A highly dangerous guy, in my opinion. He lives in this house in Bornhagen, Thuringia. The Antifa brought protests to this very rural village, and even planned a so-called *Abrissparty* (a "destruction party," in English). The police protected Höcke, and this house, because they had to. Höcke became famous for calling the Holocaust memorial a "memorial of shame for Germany." For weeks, under cover, the group Zentrum für Politische Schönheit (in English, "Centre for Political Beauty") produced a replica of the Holocaust memorial, and acquired or rented the house adjacent to Höcke's where they covered the terrain with the replica. They opened it this Monday. It's suddenly a dangerous situation now for the people who did it. The owner of this house didn't know anything about the project. The Zentrum für Politische Schönheit probably went to the owner and asked for a studio for sculptures for something like that. As of Monday, the whole project went viral.

  At the moment in Germany, and I can imagine also in Sweden, there's a long debate about how we should deal with this far-right movement. Shall we talk with them, shall we ignore them, shall we fight them and punch them? I'm more and more fascinated with the Bornhagen project by the Zentrum für Politische Schönheit because their answer to the question "How to deal with fascists?," is neither dialogue nor violence but building: a piece of architecture as a political statement.

And with that I would like to finish. Thank you very much.

MM   While working on this project and its mapping together, we discussed that it could potentially be problematic if one was to use the same kind of tools or language, such as the producing of lists and so on, that the right-wing extremists or populists are using. Could you please elaborate on this?

ST   I can talk about it, but I don't have the answer yet. Obviously fascists love lists—lists of people who they want to get rid of, sooner or later. The question now is, is it a counter strategy to also produce lists, make them public, and to do something with the houses there? My position is that only the far right turns living, the so-called private living, into a political message. A message of an ethnically cleansed community, so what the far right calls "metapolitics" is a already political project. I think the opposition "private vs. public" doesn't work when we talk about far-right extremists. Even a house by Björn Höcke is a political statement, and that's why I think there are good reasons to attack people like Höcke in their "private spheres" too, not only in the public—not physically of course, but in a smart way, like Zentrum für politische Schönheit has done it.

Question One   From a Swedish perspective, you see right-wing movements as open and placed within suburban areas. You've presented castles and where the people with power in these movements live, but what about all the followers of these movements? Have you done any research on these people?

ST   You're talking about the kind of silent voters in suburbia?

Question One (continued)   Yes. Or in villages. It's not that everyone moves to the countryside in big estates. A lot of them are in apartments coming back and forth from short prison sentences, sharing flats. This is very true in a Stockholm perspective. You can see it very clearly in the right-wing movements.

ST   I think both Markus and I are, at the moment, at a position where we have to decide between research and activism. I think to come back to your question "have you done any research on these people." I read about them but I didn't do sociological research with them, with interviews etcetera. I imagine the problems, and I can imagine what you want to say ...

MM   To add to what Stephan said already: these places are all private spaces, but one aspect they have in common, and which takes them out of the discourse of private homes and secure spaces, is that they are strategically and deliberately used as platforms. They're private homes but people come there for certain events that can't take place in "normal" public spaces.

Let's use the Antifa list or any right-wing extremist list of places and legally private persons as an example. In this case it's more about a house as a territory, which is legally private but actually used for other reasons. This is the distinction of home where three people, for whatever reason, live together and start to politically influence each other, but don't have a larger function within the discourse.

Question One (continued)   Still, if you're interested in change I wonder what space we should look at?

ST   Short term change has to reduce problems and attack individual people, not physically but on a symbolic level, like the Zentrum did with Höcke. I think every AfD politician after this event thinks twice about calling the Holocaust memorial a memorial of shame because now, this might have consequences, not only for yourself, but also for your family. It's a warning basically, but an almost poetic warning with tough consequences. The long-term change you might talk about is obviously a very complex political and economic project.

Question Two — Regarding gender—maybe it's just coincidental, but two lectures speaking about right-wing power have mostly referenced men. I'm wondering, if we've opened up the discussion of class, where are the women in this conversation, and why is it not being discussed more in regards to violent masculinism?

ST   I mentioned Marine Le Pen and Les Brigandes, but I think right-wing extremism is mainly a male problem. Many women are part of that unfortunately—in acts of stupidity, comfort, since it's sometimes simply convenient to subordinate yourself, or self-hatred, many women choose to participate in this form of patriarchal dominance. But on top of the pyramid of power of ideology is male masculinity, and the role of women is primarily reproduction, biological reproduction.

MM   Thanks, Stephan. Let's move on to the next speaker, Christina Varvia. Christina is speaking as the last person today not to underline this masculinism we just talked about, but rather because she's the only one of our three guests who will speak about design as a propositional and productive tool. How can design practice be used in order to uncover and unpack certain realities, even through technical, software-based questions?

The NSU Case
Christina Varvia

Thanks, Markus. Hi everyone, my name is Christina Varvia.

I am here to present the work of Forensic Architecture. We are a research agency based at Goldsmiths, University of London. We started as an academic research project with an award grant from the European Union. We subsequently started taking on projects as an agency where we use architecture for forensic analysis.

But how is architecture related to forensics? Most contemporary warfare is happening in cities. Whereas in the past war was conducted out in open battlefields, now very often buildings are the sites where people die, often when buildings collapse on them. Therefore, knowing and understanding how buildings work, how materials work, and how cities operate, architects are better positioned to determine what has happened within a specific violent event. The first stage in forensic architecture is to read a building and to understand what has happened, based on the ruins. What was the cause of a building's collapse?

The problem is however, that very often we do not have access to the site. What we have are images. In 2014, during the war in Gaza, we undertook a project with Amnesty International. Neither Amnesty nor Forensic Architecture were allowed to enter into Gaza, but we did have hundreds of thousands of images and videos. On one hand we needed to study the architecture that was damaged in order to figure out what happened during the offensive, but on the other hand, we couldn't visit the site. Architecture was mediatized through photographs and videos. So in instances like these we become not only a spatial practice but also a media practice that interrogates how violent events have been inscribed upon media.

We grew from a small research project to become a team of now twelve people. Our team includes architects, but also artists, filmmakers, programmers, investigative journalists, scientists, writers, etcetera. Whatever it takes, really. The way that we work is to start from small individual cases such as this one and then expand outwards to connect this event to larger policies. We do spatial and media analysis that we then present as evidence to different legal or political forms. We work with human rights groups and NGOs, and always for human rights cases where there have been state crimes. We don't take commissions from governments. On the contrary, we usually work with citizen groups, human rights groups, and the affected communities that have suffered from state violence. Although the science of forensics is usually employed by the state to investigate its people, in our practice we turn it on its back. We invert the forensic gaze and monitor state violations from a citizen perspective.

Our projects vary. The Gaza project was looking at one day of war, August 1, 2014, in the town of Rafah which was heavily bombed following the capture of an Israeli soldier. [fig.16] We were looking at hundreds of strikes within this one day. In other cases we might be looking at only one specific bombing. In the case of Miranshah in North Waziristan, we were looking at just one drone strike. We analyzed a forty-three second video clip, the only proof of the US drone strike that reportedly killed four people. We analyzed the site of the strike based on that footage: the black space was what was not covered by the video, the white was were image was available, and we marked the shrapnel marks. By connecting these marks we figured out where the device detonated.

This [fig.17] is the case of the forty-three disappeared students of Ayotzinapa, in Mexico. There are multiple narratives of what happened on this event. These were gathered in an independent expert report which we had to datamine and analyze each account in relation to location and time. We then plotted all of those narratives on an online platform as well as on this timeline, in order to detect contradictions and discrepancies on the accounts. The different colors represent the different accounts: the official government's narrative is in black—the students' narrative in red, the police in blue, the military in green, and the cartels in purple. What

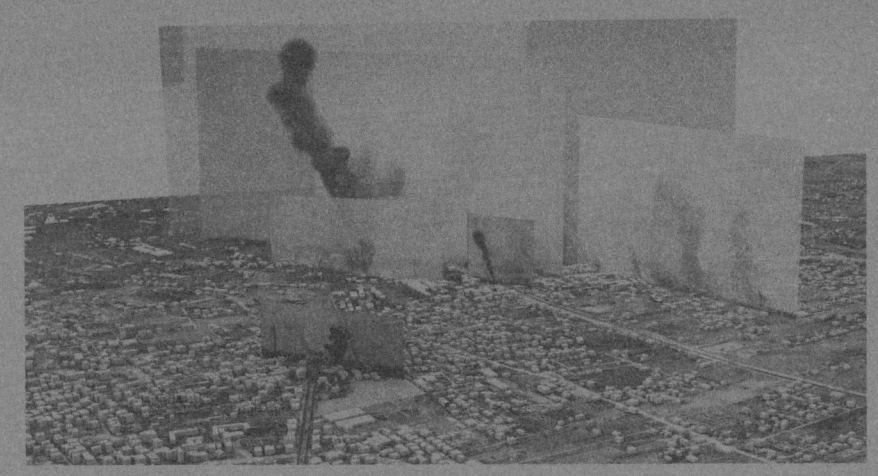

16

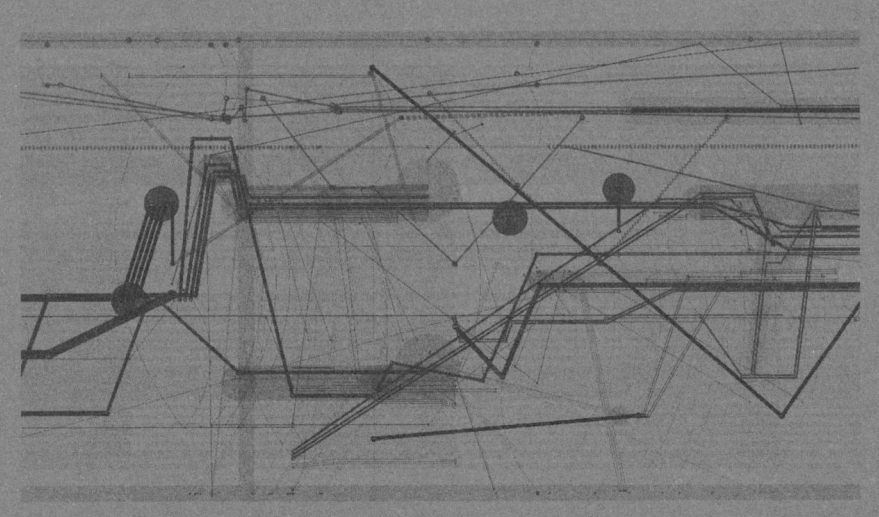

17

we created was essentially a research tool to enable more researchers as well as the families of the disappeared students to investigate the events. So, our work varies in scale, topic and method.

In the context of this wonderful event today, I will focus on the NSU investigation. This is the investigation of the murder of young Halit Yozgat by members of the NSU. Halit was living in Kassel, in Germany, and used to work in his father's internet cafe. He was the ninth victim out of ten racist murders, targeting mostly people with a Turkish background, which took place between 2000 and 2007 all across Germany. The murders were conducted by the so-called NSU, the National Socialist Underground, which allegedly only consists of three people. The NSU murdered people who were running small successful businesses in Germany and they always used the same gun. Two of them, Uwe Mundlos and Uwe Boehnhardt, have now committed suicide, and Beate Zschäpe, the last surviving member is currently on trial.

For a long time, the police were mostly considering people of the Turkish community as suspects. They were calling the murders "Döner murders," a racist way of framing them as the result of Turkish mafia. They were interrogating and harassing the victims' family members, considering them as suspects, instead of looking at racist motives. Following the ninth murder, the murder of Halit, the families of the victims organized two big demonstrations in Kassel and Dortmund. They demanded that the government recognize these murders as a series of racist murders and that they be protected as German-Turkish citizens. These protests led to a series of civil society initiatives that promoted awareness of the up-and-coming neo-Nazi scene. However, the local, situated knowledge was ignored, and it wasn't until the NSU themselves claimed that they were responsible for the murders that the racist motive was accepted by the German state. So this was a complete and utter failure of the state to protect its people and to recognize what these murders were really about. Even on the current court case in Munich that is trying Beate Zschäpe and five people who could have aided the NSU, questions of structural and infrastructural racism are not included. The question of why the German government failed to protect its own citizens is not answered. In 2015 some of the civil-society initiatives formed a coalition called "Unraveling the NSU Complex." They organized a citizen tribunal and commissioned us to examine the case of Halit.

We were asked to investigate the murder of Halit because of one person who was present in the internet cafe during the time of the murder. Andreas Temme was a secret service agent for the Hessian Secret Service, the Verfassungsschutz, investigating and gathering intelligence about the far-right movement. Even though he is a representative of the state, he was working within the police department, he did not come forward as a witness. He was eventually recognized from his internet login data. He had logged in an online dating site called ilove.de with the codename "wildman70." He was consequently brought forward and said "I was in the wrong place and the wrong time, I didn't notice anything. It was really unfortunate, but sorry I don't remember anything from the event." However all other five witnesses in the café had heard something. They didn't recognize it was a murder, but they did hear a loud sound, they noticed something.

We came in 2016, after there was a big leak of court documents that were published online in 2015 by a group called NSU leaks. They released photographs of the crime scene and witness testimonies, as well as a really precious document: a video of Andreas Temme himself reenacting his visit to the internet cafe for the police. The police asked him to show them how could he have moved through the internet cafe and not have noticed anything.

Starting from this, we started by reconstructing a 3-D model of the internet cafe based on the available images. The internet cafe is no longer there, it has been remodeled. It is now a shop selling honey. We used the available images, measurements and descriptions from the family who owned the cafe to build the space as a digital model, as well as a 1:1 physical reconstruction of the crime scene. For the physical model we abstracted the 3-D model, created a scaffold structure and reconstructed the key spaces of the crime scene in order to do a series of experiments. We used only the surfaces which were important for our investigation, for example glass panels that would have reflected the sound of gunshots, tables which would have obstructed one's vision in the café etc. [fig.18] We built it at the House of World Cultures [HKW] in Berlin, who partly funded this work. The experiments had to do mostly

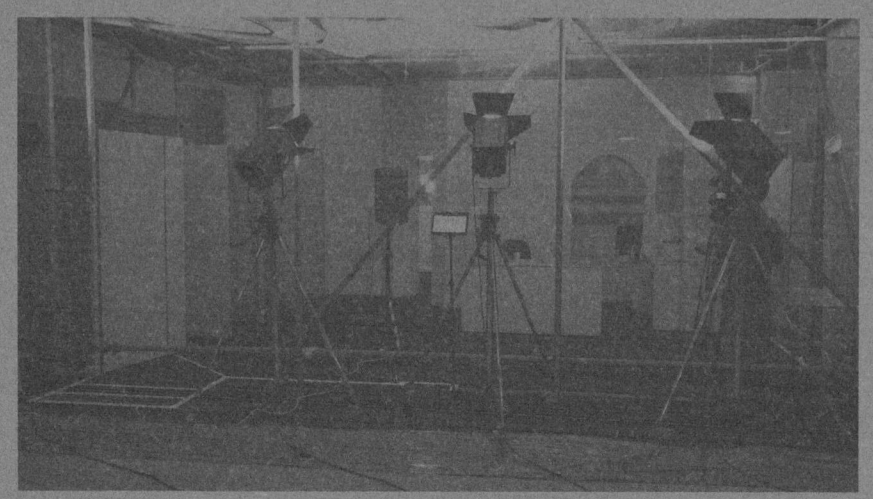

18

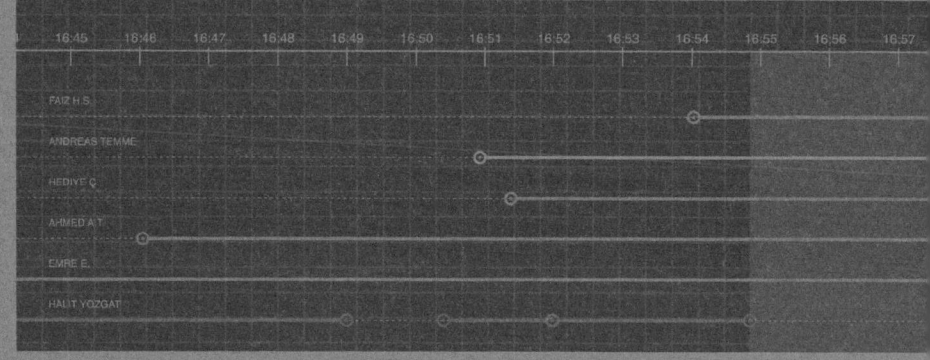

19

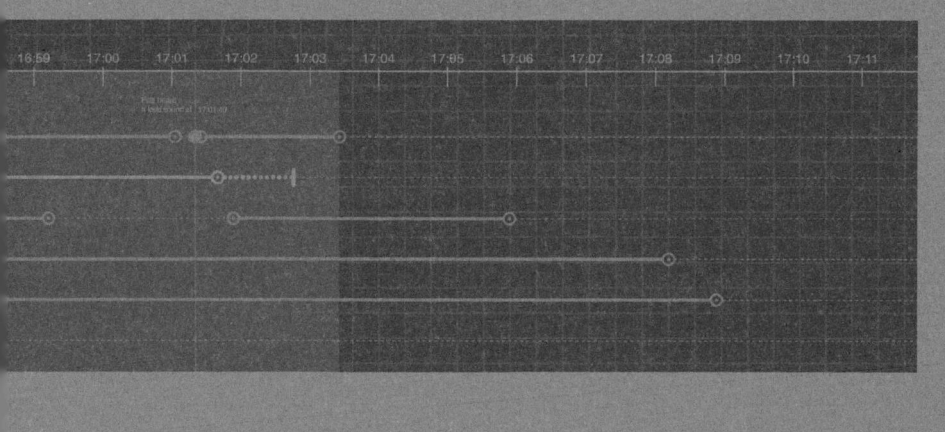

with trying to answer the questions: was Temme involved in the case, did he witness it, and if so why didn't he come forward?

This is important—we chose to investigate this case because it is the one of the ten murders where you have a state representative in the crime scene. By analyzing his account, his testimony based on his reenactment, we are able to prove that he in fact witnessed the event. Then, this small fact starts to unravel a whole series of questions about why he lied, why the state protected him, why is he still working as a state employee, and eventually, how is the state involved in this series of murders? Why did they fail to protect these people, and what are they covering? His presence in this space is the key through which we try to activate this political back and forth.

We conducted a series of tests that have to do with timing, in terms of when he moved in and out, and with the three senses. Could he have heard the gunshots, could he have smelled the gunpowder, as he left he internet cafe, could he have seen the body of Halit when he was leaving?

The interesting part about a murder happening in an internet cafe is that everyone is logged in. There were five witnesses [fig.19] marked out here, and we know when they logged in and when they logged out. This is our main infrastructure, our Cambridge Analytica equivalent if you will. Witness testimonies are often abstract, in terms of timing. But people do remember what they were doing during an event, when they heard a loud sound. For example, one of the witnesses said she was on the phone to her brother, we know this was her second phone call. So we know that when she heard the loud sound it was somewhere between this time frame. This is the timeline of another witness playing Call of Duty, a popular game where players shoot Nazis—the irony is explicit here. And so again, the timeline and model for us is the infrastructure through which the time-space narrative plays out.

Temme's login and logout is quite important because he says that perhaps he could have left before the murder happened. We have looked at the absolute time frame of when this murder could have taken place. Faiz, the only witness who is in the front part of the cafe where the murder takes place, was also the last person who spoke to Halit. Faiz entered his phone booth at this time and when he came out the murder had already taken place. So this is our absolute time frame. Within this time frame we need to figure out where Andreas Temme was and whether he was able to witness the event.

According to his reenactment video, which we treat as Temme's testimony given with the language of his body, we have the duration of his exit, how long it took him to leave the internet café after he logged out. (We noticed how, in his reenactment, he took care not to look toward where Halit was found dead.) The question is, at the time of the murder, was he in the back room, in the front room, or had he already left?

In the first scenario, there would be thirty-nine seconds from the time that he left until the time that the witness, Faiz finished his phone-call and came out. It becomes quite technical, but we start with a series of reenactments that we conduct in the real scale model with volunteer actors where we test whether thirty-nine seconds are enough for following series of events to happen.

First we have Temme leaving. Then we have Halit coming back. We tried to play out the last moment that they could have missed each other. Temme claimed that when he left there was no one at the front desk and he couldn't find Halit anywhere, so for that scenario to be true it would mean that Halit would have to be already out somewhere. Of course there was no other witness who claimed that Halit ever left the shop and no one saw him outside. For the purpose of this scenario, we assume that he had left so then he would have to come back, the murderer would follow him in, and here we're measuring steps again. After that, the witness that is in the phone booth comes out. This whole sequence takes thirty-five seconds, which means there's only four seconds left for them to miss each other. However this is in a highly coordinated environment where we're giving precise instructions—but things don't happen like that. Finally one witness testimony excludes that scenario altogether because they report the gunshots earlier on.

Specifically, we go back into the testimonies and look at when people reported the gunshots. Here we see one of the witnesses who is in this space between the two rooms, just next to Halit's desk where he was murdered. She hears the gunshots at this particular time when she's talking, as she said, on the phone to her brother. Then there's another witness who says he was inputting the pin number for a second phone call and that's when he heard the gunshots. This is quite an important moment because we know it's right before that second phone call came through. It becomes quite technical. We figure out how long it takes for someone to type in eight digits on a keypad. And based on these two accounts we figured out that there's an absolute time frame, and the gunshots were fired within this frame.

This means that Temme's claim that he might have left the café when the murder happened, "Scenario One," needs to be disregarded, because the witnesses are actually stating that the murder took place in a completely different time frame.

The second scenario is whether it is possible that Temme was in front of the cafe when the murder took place. The data set that we were using at the time implied that this was possible, which also means that he would have confronted, come face to face, with the killer. We later found out that this was not the case, and that the only scenario that was viable was scenario three, where Temme was sitting in the back room logged in when the murder took place. This is the scenario that we dedicated most of our work on, and it's important because it follows these three questions:

Temme claims he didn't notice anything. He said "I didn't hear anything, I didn't smell anything, I didn't see anything." He even said "It's surprising to me because I am used to handling guns," because he is a gun enthusiast. "I'm sure I would have noticed something," he said. So we consider this testimony. The crime that we're investigating is not necessarily whether he was part of the murder, the question is whether he was lying in court when he said he hadn't witnessed anything. Was he committing the crime of perjury?

We start with a basic question: could he hear the gunshot? A Česká 83 with a makeshift silencer was used for the murder. We worked with ballistic weapons experts who went to Arizona and shot this gun as well as three guns of the same calibre. They measured the sound level that these weapons produced, and applied a silencer on one of the guns and measured the suppression of the sound. We then had a very accurate sound signature of the gun with the silencer. None of those gunshots, even with a silencer, was lower than 130 decibels. We then positioned a loud speaker in the position of the killer in the 1:1 model and we played the gunshot in space. All the materials that were used for the installation were specified by acoustic consultants who made sure the materials were behaving similar to the original crime scene. Then we measured the sound levels from Temme's perspective, sitting on PC 2 on the other side of the cafe. There's an open doorway between the two spaces, and so the sound was measured somewhere between ninety-four and ninety-nine decibels. The sound was so loud in the space that it was shocking to everyone who was present. We also corroborated this with digital models doing ray tracing analysis. We were working with acoustic consultants as we mapped out exactly how much sound is attenuated by space and the architecture of the crime scene, how it bounces off surfaces and how the materials absorb or amplify the sound waves. Lastly, we created a digital model of our 1:1 installation and run the same tests in order to corroborate both models. This is the ground truth model that calibrates our digital simulation and physical experimentation. We were able to determine that for one eighth of a second, the sound of the gun was as loud as that of a jackhammer drilling concrete.

We move further than that into a smell analysis. For the smell analysis we worked with a fluid dynamics expert from Imperial College. In the physical model we used a smoke machine in order to visualize the volume of gases produced by two gunshots of the specific ammunition. We superimposed Temme's movement according to his reenactment video within this dissipation of gases. Further on, we conducted a digital simulation with our fluid dynamics expert who designed an algorithm that traces the movement of particles in space. We calculated the threshold of perception of ammonia particles, one of the byproducts of the bullet combustion. The threshold of perception is marked in blue. [fig.20]

It is interesting to consider space not only from a basic architectural understanding, as the scene of a crime, but also as a volume of particles. The sensory space becomes something of a cloud that one is either within or outside of. As the killer opened and closed the door to exit, he created a small vortex which mixed the particles of ammonia, evened them out within the space. We were trying to figure out: could he have noticed it? We figured out

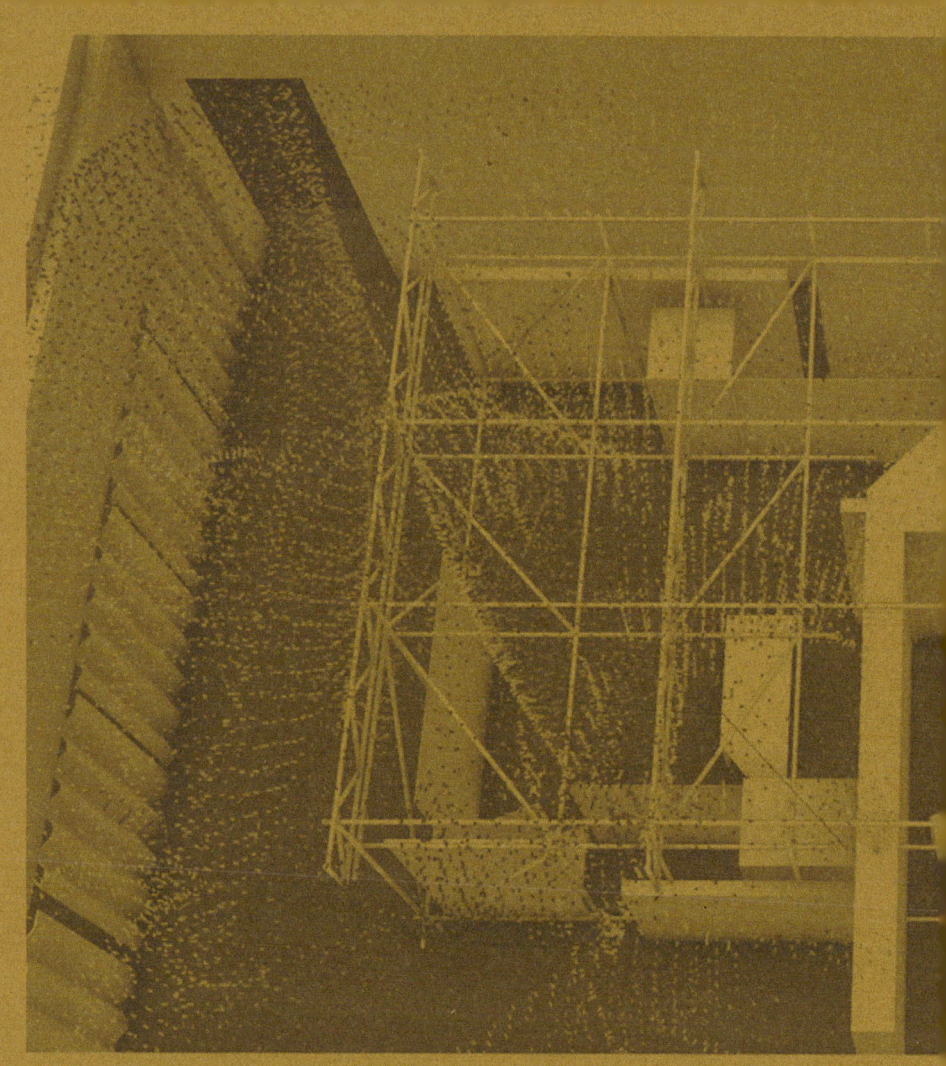

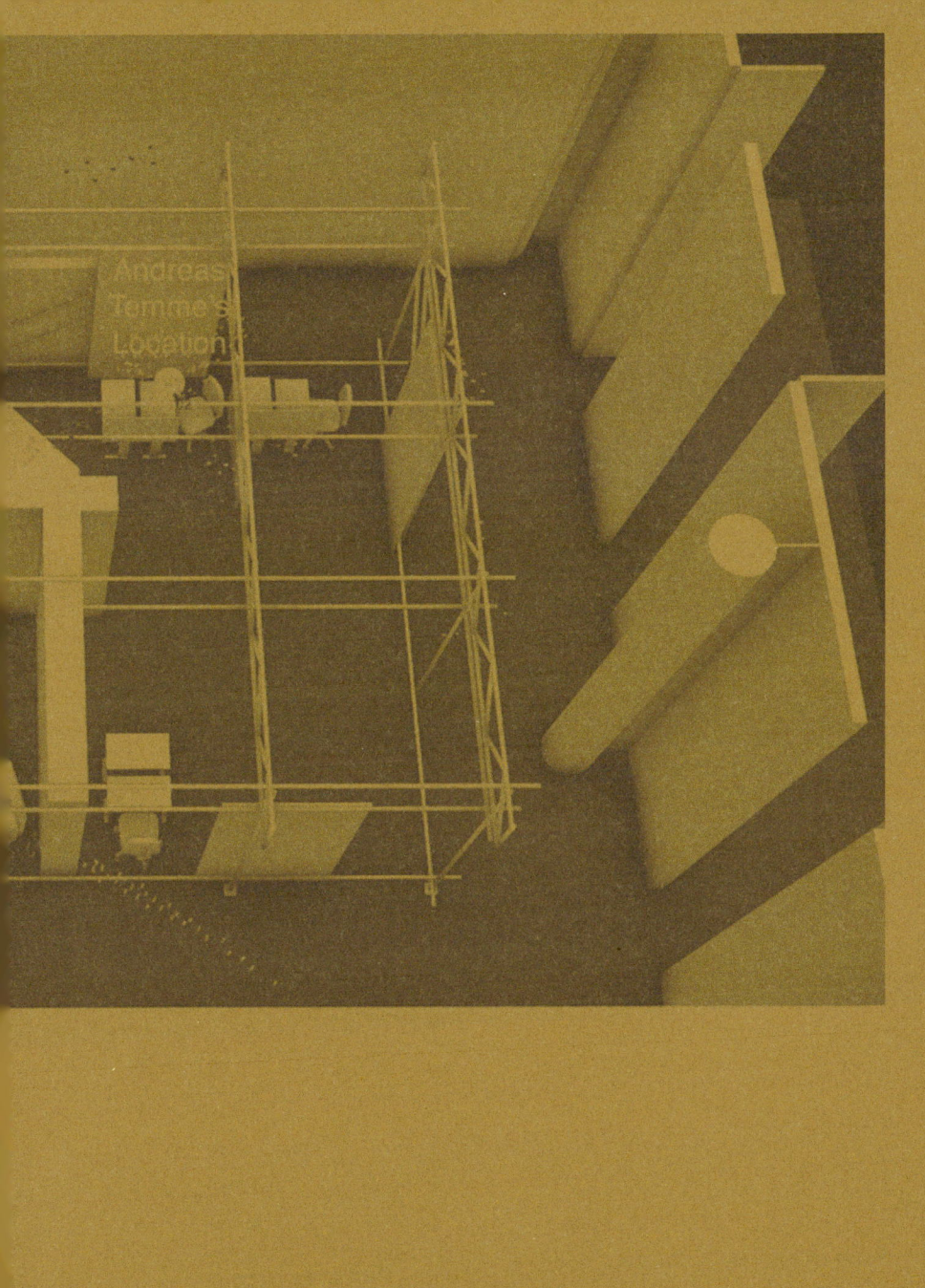

that if Temme left within the first twenty seconds after the killer fired his two shots, he would have walked right into this cloud of smell. If Temme left twenty seconds later, then we don't know, because we cannot be sure of the original recipe of the ammunition. We called different companies who make these specific bullets and the ammo for the bullets but they wouldn't tell us. Still, we mapped out the ammonia particles because according to a few scientific papers, this is a standard by-product of bullets of this range.

The last experiment we did was a vision experiment where we simulated Temme's point of view from the moment that he logged out of the chatting website, and how he exited the internet café, according to his own testimony. [fig.21] We are only considering whether, according to his own account, he could have missed seeing the body of Halit. Therefore, we're trying to figure out whether the police investigation was sufficient and whether they were right to believe his testimony when he said he didn't notice anything. Looking at his reenactment one can note that even though he is supposed to be looking for Halit in order to pay him, he is not ever turning his gaze to the desk where he expects to find Halit. Most importantly, we are looking at this moment when he places a coin on the front desk, to pay for his visit, and behind that desk Halit is lying dead.

We reenacted his movement with an actor in the 1:1 model. At first, we didn't tell the actor, that we were going to have a person lying in Halit's position. The actor was shocked when he saw someone lying behind the counter. We also tested every possible body position that Halit could have fallen in. Halit's father, told us how he found his son, as he was the first one to have discovered him dead — but we also tried falling in different ways to see if it would even be possible that Halit would fall in such a way that he would not be visible when someone leaned over the desk. Temme is almost 190 cm tall, and the desk was only 70 cm high, so the experiment was damning.

We undertook this tedious work in order to crack open the involvement of a government agent. Within this one shop, these seventy-seven square meters of the internet cafe, different actors come together. There's a neo-Nazi killer, a murder victim, a member of the police, and members of immigrant communities living in

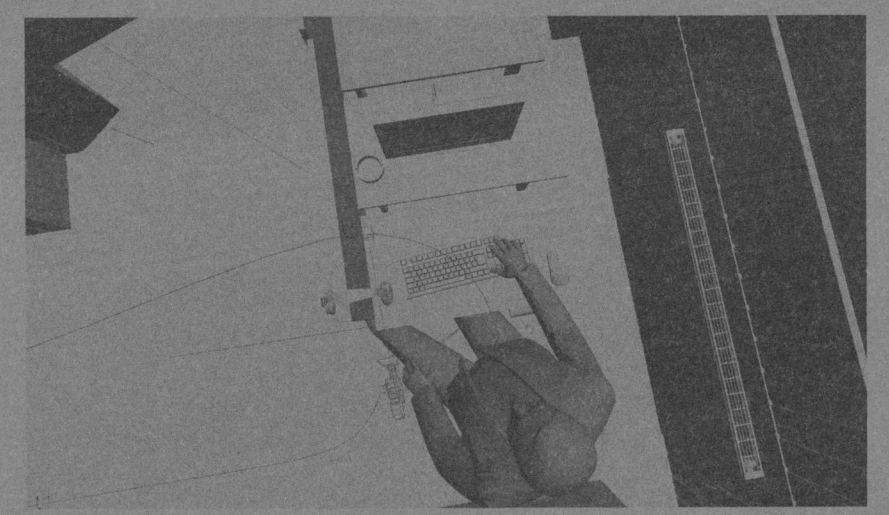

Europe—all in the same place. The crime scene becomes a nexus through which we try to unravel these complex relationships, and critique the role of the state and its failure to protect its people.

I'll finish this presentation by describing the life that the project has had in different forums. We originally presented the preliminary results in a press conference, on April 6, 2017, which was the eleventh anniversary of Halit's death this year. Following that, we were invited to submit our preliminary results to the Federal State Parliamentary Commission of Inquiry that was underway for this case. We submitted our results at the time when the Commission of Inquiry was wrapping up their investigation, so our results were added as an addendum, to be considered in later examinations. After this we presented our final results to the People's Tribunal "Unraveling the NSU Complex" that was organized in Cologne. This was a completely self organized event organized by different civil society initiatives that formed a coalition. They interrogated the murders in different ways, examining the deep history of racism, and they were also the ones who commissioned our investigation. Then we presented the work as a video installation at documenta 14. This was important, because the murder was in Kassel, and documenta was happening in Kassel just a few hundred meters from the actual crime scene. We were able to bring the whole investigation back to the place where it all started and to draw in a huge audience. It's really difficult to get people interested in stories like that through publication, or any kind of human rights report that NGOs tend to write. Amnesty International, Human Rights Watch, all these organizations write these beautiful reports and after they publish them they sit on a shelf because they are quite heavy documents to read—there's just not enough people reading them. By exhibiting this in documenta we put this work in the public sphere and in the art sphere. It drew the attention of hundreds of people, and that created political pressure. Following this, we also published a report which analyzes our methodology, and credits the team and experts who worked with us. We were also invited to submit the results to the Hessian State Commission of Inquiry, so we submitted the video and our report. On August 25, 2017, our investigation was presented in front of Temme at the Hessian Inquiry—he was confronted by this work.

He was shown the video and was asked to respond to this study that very clearly states he was a witness to the murder. He said, "Well, that doesn't bring any memories back, but I am all over this footage, do they have the right to use my image?" His argument was mostly about copyright.

The same day that the report was presented by the SPD party in front of Temme, the CDU, the Christian Democrat Party, presented a counter-report to our report in the same Parliamentary Commission of Inquiry in Hessen. They marked up our report with comments like "spurious allegations," "this is unclear," "inaccurate," etcetera. However, the CDU's critique was unsigned, so we don't know who wrote it and we don't know what credentials did the author have to be fitted to analyze our report, a report that conducted by a university based research agency working with very specific expert consultants.

So a political party, the CDU, presented this counter-report and offered no explanation, no backing for their critique. They were just trying to discredit the work. And here is a really interesting moment, the moment when the research project becomes the subject of critical debate within a political forum. Another thing that came with their argumentation—other than the petty notes on the language of the report—was that we are an artist group, therefore they don't have to take our investigation into consideration. We answered of course by directing them to our credentials, and asked back to see the expertise of those critiquing us and determining that those results are inaccurate.

They also said—and this was the most fruitful part—that we based some of our results to a data set that is no longer accurate. This is something that is really interesting, because we were working from the leaked documents, from whatever was already in the public domain. There seemed to be a second police report by a different police unit, that resulted to different log in data. This was a report that only a few people had access to within the political sphere. The timings were a little different. But their critique, revealed to us the newest data, which actually confirms the fact that Temme should have been in the back of the cafe still logged in when the murder took place. Therefore he was definitely a witness, according to our sensory experiments. What you see in the back and forth in this project, is that a research project that exists within a university can create this backlash, conversation, and dialogue when it becomes active in all these forums. Even within the hurtful moment when we had to admit that our data was wrong, it was a fruitful moment because the opposing voice presented to us the tools through which we can reassess the work. We integrated the new data, and then were able to fight back. The question of the involvement of Temme still remains. None of those arguments changes the result that Temme was a witness to a neo-Nazi murder.

Finally, the CDU's last critique was that we had not taken into account the "psychology of perception." This is an interesting philosophical moment for us as well, because of course we are all arguing for what truth really is; we are preoccupied with the construction of the truth, and we problematize the idea that any kind of evidence needs to be constructed in order to be understood. On the other hand there is also a very clear distinction between the truth and a lie. It might be difficult to say what the truth is, but it's very easy to say what a lie is. This is why, as a research process, we usually start by debunking the falsehoods of the official narrative.

We published an open letter as a response to the CDU's counter-report and engaged in this argument of the "psychology of perception." We asked to see evidence of Temme's psychological state that proves that he would have missed gunshots as loud as these. Beyond a certain level sound can wake you up from sleep, therefore even if Temme was unconscious he would have woken up. If the CDU claims that Temme could have missed the sound of the gunshots due to psychological reasons, then we are challenging them to present proof that Temme was indeed mentally ill. Then the question becomes why is he still employed, why is he still working for the state, and why does the state protect him? Even though this case proves that he's the worst spy there could have been! And yet he is employed. So our final argument has to do with incompetence and demands accountability for who the state employs.

It's an interesting game we're playing. It is very rigorous and tedious at times, it becomes rhetoric and dialectic at others. To consider this example alongside the other practices that were presented today suggests the ways in which each of us operate in the political sphere with whatever skills we have available. It's not that our skills are so specific, they are, from an architecture point of view, quite a ubiquitous toolkit. But the reappropriation of those tools for the purposes of investigative practices is something we have found to have great potential.

To close, I would just like to mention another neo-Nazi case that we're working on. We are currently investigating the murder of Pavlos Fyssas, a young Greek antifascist rapper, who was attacked and then executed by Golden Dawn members in Athens. Here we are working directly with the lawyers of the victim's family. What's interesting is that the trial puts a whole political party on the stand. Golden Dawn has seats in the parliament, but it also operates as a criminal organization — there's almost too much evidence to prove that. If the trial proves that they're a criminal organization, Golden Dawn has to leave the parliament. So it's a really important moment to see how those forums get activated, from the legal forum to the political forum.

Even though it was known that Golden Dawn had a racist agenda, there could not have been a confrontation in the Greek parliament if there is no crime. In the Greek parliament, one cannot argue against ideology. You need to argue against actions. So even though everyone knew Golden Dawn were Nazis, there was no way to argue against an ideology, against what people believe is right or wrong. Unfortunately there had to be a murder and a series of attacks for that whole legal mechanism to come into play.

The way that we are working in this case is similar, to the NSU case: it's unpacking this one moment where ideology and all forces are crystallized. We are investigating the role of the police. We try to draw outwards, toward understanding institutional racism and the whole infrastructural networks that allow those kind of murders to happen. There were eight police officers who were present at the crime scene and although they admit that they were witnesses, they said they were too late, they could not have prevented the murder. We know that they the police are sympathetic to Golden Dawn. So we are challenging their statement. Again, we are focusing on this one event to figure out how it extends toward a vaster network.

This is where I leave you. Thank you.

November 25, 2017

MM   Thank you so much, Christina. This was interesting and a very important contribution and endnote in regard to the potential practice-based approach to the subject. In terms of your work concerning the NSU, will the project be continued from your end?

CV   Any time when we have an opportunity we try to push. In the open letter that we published in the summer, we asked to be invited to the Hessian Parliamentary Commission of Inquiry so that we can push forward, since there has been a critique about our report we would like to argue and debate in the same forum. That's what is happening at the moment. We're just waiting for the next moment where we will be able to apply some pressure.

MM   Any direct questions from the audience?

Question One   What would you say are the main drawbacks working as an artistic group in this way, addressing politics?

CV   That's an interesting question. We're not an artistic group per se. We're a research group, but we do have artists who are acting as investigators within our group. This is something that we own up to and engage with. So when you talk about the way the environment registers information, somehow aesthetic practitioners are the best-suited people to do this kind of work. The simplest example is if some information is missed between the frames of a film, a filmmaker would know that there's around twenty-five frames per second. There might be less, there might be up until sixty. If a bullet travels faster than that, you might have missed it, or it might only be caught within a frame. So you can understand the relationship between time and the medium that has captured the event.

We are considering everyone's skill set as an opening, a starting point, and we're trying to see how everyone can be an expert in their own way, in their own right, including people who have embodied knowledge. In the case of the NSU, the families knew before the state knew that this was a series of racist murders, because they have an understanding of this context different from what the police would see. We are considering everyone as an expert in their own right, and we defend our right to argue for events and truths within those events, on that basis. Of course the drawback is, as you've seen, that we might be dismissed as an artist group. But this is the point where we just bring forward all the cases that we've worked on, the fact that they've been admitted to the UN and different civil courts, used by different lawyers throughout. Anyone's credibility is built with some example or precedent I guess.

Question Two

Thank you for a very interesting presentation. I think that this case of artist group or researchers is quite an interesting thing, because I think the legitimacy is based partly institutional—that you can say you're a research group within a university makes you more legitimate than if you were a freestanding artist. This points to how truth and knowledge production often work in a larger institutional framework, while other groups are ignored. So it's quite interesting to look at those aspects because they are also political. I think you would not come this far if you were an independent artist. So you're totally dependent on the university.

Question Three

But while there is a lot of truth to your comment, we're also now seeing successful examples of different tactics being used by people who don't belong to formal institutions. Maybe because that gives them freedom. Many artists have resources and different opportunities to do investigative journalism, or research-based art practices, directly politically

	engaged work that blurs art and action.
Question Two (continued)	The question is where you can operate. It's a great discussion, because you can operate in that field in media, but directly if you went to the court that institutional thing becomes more important. Media now, in any case, is taking over the court system, which is kind of problematic.

CV   Let's say we could have done the same exact work without being in a university, but it might not have been received the same way.

Question Four	You mentioned that they criticized you for not getting the "psychological aspects" of perception—I think that's absolutely ridiculous! I'm a psychologist of perception. Audio itself is a type of event, over any threshold, and smell—you can't account for vision, it's true we don't know where he looked—but you can't close your ears and you can't close your nose. Particularly somebody who knows about gunpowder. It's ridiculous.

CV   Absolutely.

Question Four (continued)	All your investigations have a time lag—they are coming afterwards, as far as I know your work. Have you any ongoing context or this sort of starting investigations where, say, the gunpowder is not there yet? Proactive forensics?

CV   It's a bit of a tricky game I would say, in the same way that you would consider predictive forensics from the police to be problematic. Then you move into the whole issue of the CIA having lists of people they consider to be potential terrorists and prosecuting them before the crime has happened. There's a moment where you have to step back and say, OK, shouldn't we allow the benefit of the doubt for someone? From my perspective, you can't prosecute someone before they've done a crime.

  The closest we have done is try to do something very fast afterwards. And that is interesting when you look at Syria. We had one case where there was a US bombing of a mosque. The Pentagon denied it was a mosque, and for us it was a very easy exercise to check whether it was a religious building. The question was then: how fast can we do it? We did it in two and a half weeks. We analyzed the building according to images the Pentagon had published about the bombing strike. There was a drone image, and we cross referenced that to different images of the building before it was struck to prove that it was actually a religious building. We showed where people gathered. We combined that with testimony, and then the Pentagon had to accept the fact that, yes, they targeted a religious building. And this is, let's say, not before an event, but considering that there's an active operation happening in Syria at the moment, the work that we can do monitoring attacks as soon as they happen influences policy and goes back into it. There's groups like AirWars—they're not architects, they're journalists, but they monitor Russian and US coalition strikes in Syria and Iraq and just by counting civilian casualties and publishing reports they monitor them, and continuously contact all of those big powers who are active in the operations in Syria and Iraq. The moment there's a spike and they call it out, there needs to be a response. This is the role of the watchdog, of always being out there, monitoring registering and reporting back—that for me is the closest you could go to being really part of game as it is developing right now. Trying to prevent it.

Question Five   *You* are observing *them*. Has it influenced you, when they start observing you? As a researcher? How does that play into your profession?

CV Everything we do is kind of public, but we have had this question before. I think that we're still quite small, that we're not a legitimate target yet to be sabotaged or to be tampered with. That being said, we're also not naive, we probably know that there's some surveillance on us and they know everything that we're doing anyway. Does that answer your question?

HG Did you ask whether the actions of Forensic Architecture are actually changing the actions of the German police investigating the case, because they're anticipating these moves?

Question Five (continued) No, I'm asking about your development as professionals. It's really scary, you have all been talking about intimidations.

MM This is a really important question to bring up, and unites all of these different practices. The question is basically do you feel that you are becoming a target by doing that particular work?

CV I haven't felt that yet but I'm sure it's imminent. I think also the distance we have for us helps, particularly because we're in London. The German case is the first we've done in Europe, so we have had distance till now. We have been subjects of trolls and certain critiques, but never to a point where we feel a threat.

MM Another question that I wanted to ask all of you is regarding the question of mandate. At first, it seems to be quite clear—for example when I think about you, Hannes, your background is in economics but then you became a journalist. There is the Hannes, who is employed by a magazine, and then there is the Hannes, who is involved in other, self-initiated projects.

HG I just wanted to add to your question now that I got it [to earlier audience question]—sorry for being so slow. I feel this is the most important question for journalism currently, and it's complicated. I used to laugh about death threats, it's kind of a little honor, because you can't take them seriously. If he really wants to kill you he can. Times have profoundly changed, because you can basically kill people, information-wise. You cannot only terrorize them digitally but you can drive them mad. By using all sorts of strategies, and those are being used.

With the decay of the institutions like my newspaper employer, as Markus, mentioned, it's the structural support that is gone now. You get attacked with a combination of disinformation and bullying over the Internet and probably even other physical harm. Some people feel like agents, they have to carry out the thing they have read about you.

This is a time of information warfare. The problem is that "media" is actually people like me. And people like you. There is basically nobody who could save you from harm. That's very much an issue once you touch power. It's not as if my editor-in-chief would come and tell the trolls to go away. This is one of the biggest questions right now in journalism actually. If you're really there to stand out—the guys who threaten you know all these newspapers are going to close doors within the next five years. They will not be able to protect you at all. So you're basically alone.

MM Yes, this is of course the case—but at the same time an event like today and tonight proves that you are not alone. There is huge interest in, and need for your work and those very specific, varied approaches through which this subject can be tackled.

Thank you all so much for attending this event and for being such interesting conversation partners throughout the day.

And we'll move forward from here.

1
In the months since this symposium and increased news coverage of this story, Facebook introduced some ad-related transparency measures.

2
In a *New York Times* article published on May 2, 2018, Cambridge Analytica announced it would file for bankruptcy "amid growing legal and political scrutiny of its business practices and work for Donald J. Trump's presidential campaign."

3
Antifascist movements, specifically referring to the Antifascist movements in Germany.

4
AfD, Alternative für Deutschland, is a far-right political party in Germany. Since 2017, it is the largest opposition party in the German Bundestag.

Template Culture:
Parameters of Political Design Themes for the Internet

Konrad Renner

The World Wide Web is made-to-measure: it has adapted to the desires and needs of its gatekeepers. Reinforced by the technical status quo, the loose, anti-authoritarian network originally founded by scientists and the American military has over time developed visual standards. On buttons and boxes, on recurring visual patterns: <header><nav><main><footer>.

As a result, the visual interface of the internet is created in the form of templates, converted into designed and parametric interfaces for CMSes[1] such as *Wordpress*, *Drupal*, and *Typo3*. These digital templates can be arranged independently of content, and allow users to publish easily on websites. Neither programming skills nor complex graphic decisions are necessary: templates provide customized results within a programmed radius, a manifestation of the visual connection between back-end and front-end, senders and receivers.

Popular content management systems are being developed and driven by a large open source community. About twenty-five percent of all websites worldwide use Wordpress, originally intended as a blog tool, which thus represents a potential market for around 250 million plugins and themes, with commercial providers for further extensions, enhanced features and additional visual templates. These are offered for download on large platforms such as www.themeforest.net and can be found via technical parameters or search terms such as *Education*, *Wedding*, or *Political*.

The use of template-originating websites saw an unprecedented expansion in the 2016 US election, when a whole range of "political" themes emerged for different parties and positions. A local sheriff from Tennessee or a candidate for the US

Senate could use the same website template from the same online pool, with costs ranging from thirty to fifty-nine dollars for the unlimited use of one design. Such models, provided and offered for sale and download, are mostly owned by companies based in Indonesia (Theme Warrior) and Bangladesh (Trendy Theme, HasTech, Codeboxr). The providers are not specialists of political platforms exclusively, but create generic visual surfaces made up of repeated modules such as slideshows, feeds, and text-image combinations. Only visual language itself changes: colors, volumes and visual stereotypes are adapted to respective topics and are offered under other labels. Placeholder texts are also adaptable to content: "Get Off the Sidelines! Be a part of the movement and participate in building a better future for our country! Join this historical campaign and stand up for the values that make our country great. Make a difference."[2]

The linguistic adaptation of well-known pop-patriotic statements goes hand in hand with the visual language. Templates like Elections, Senate, and Frontrunner are dominated by heroic imagery, flanked by waving national flags and country-specific heraldry. Portraits of individuals placed against blurry backgrounds suggest a direct contact with the candidates—an unfiltered view. Color palettes are reduced to respective national or party colors and overstated cultural affiliations. The typographic system employed uses well-known traditional typefaces and is limited to centered core statements in the conciseness of tweets. Social channels are embedded as modules and taken out of their original visual identity. Small animations of statistics and data link the technical status quo[3] and networked action: *We are many! Be part of this (virtual) movement!*

Most importantly, such website templates provide various functions that are intended to allow a more direct, private communication between senders and receivers. The template Frontrunner uses its module to ensure that first-time visitors of the website are forwarded directly to newsletter subscription before they reach content. The website of the German national-conservative politician Beatrix von Storch offers twelve options on the first few pixels of her personal website (Wordpress' *Campaign* theme) to connect with her on other channels. Other participation options include:

"Meet Our Team," "Event Management," and various donation options, all conveying the elementary need to directly, instantly, and personally connect visitors with political actors. Personal portfolios and campaign websites offer only a first point of contact, a central hub for Google and other interested parties. Visitors are therefore to be quickly redirected to non-public, personal communication channels. In this way, they are able to participate directly in a political movement through closed Facebook groups and private accounts. This enables the growth of a dangerous trend with effects evident in populist politics from Trump to the AfD: identification through participation.[4]

Yet despite its inherent rigidity, the visual culture of templates causes blurring. Clear assignments to political parties, people, and organizations are avoided, as otherwise universal application areas would be denied and the economic effort would increase considerably. In terms of visual language and content, such sites remain sophisticated. Generic website designs have principle on the part of the providers, because they are inherent to the recycling chain of design templates. The are made to work profitably, to narrow selections, and to make things easier and less complex—for providers, designers and users. Radical positions thus masquerade as normal internet. At first glance, the websites of far-right and radical groups are visually indistinguishable from other parties, or even the next innovative IT startup. They all use the same easily accessible pools, whether knowingly or for simply economic reasons.[5]

The visual flattening of digital culture through templates and ready-made aesthetic solutions implies boredom and threatening lethargy. This means graphic design should once again make significant differences visible. Political opposites must be tangible, readable, and made accessible to the widest possible audience to unmask right-wing propaganda and hate speech within the visual mainstream.

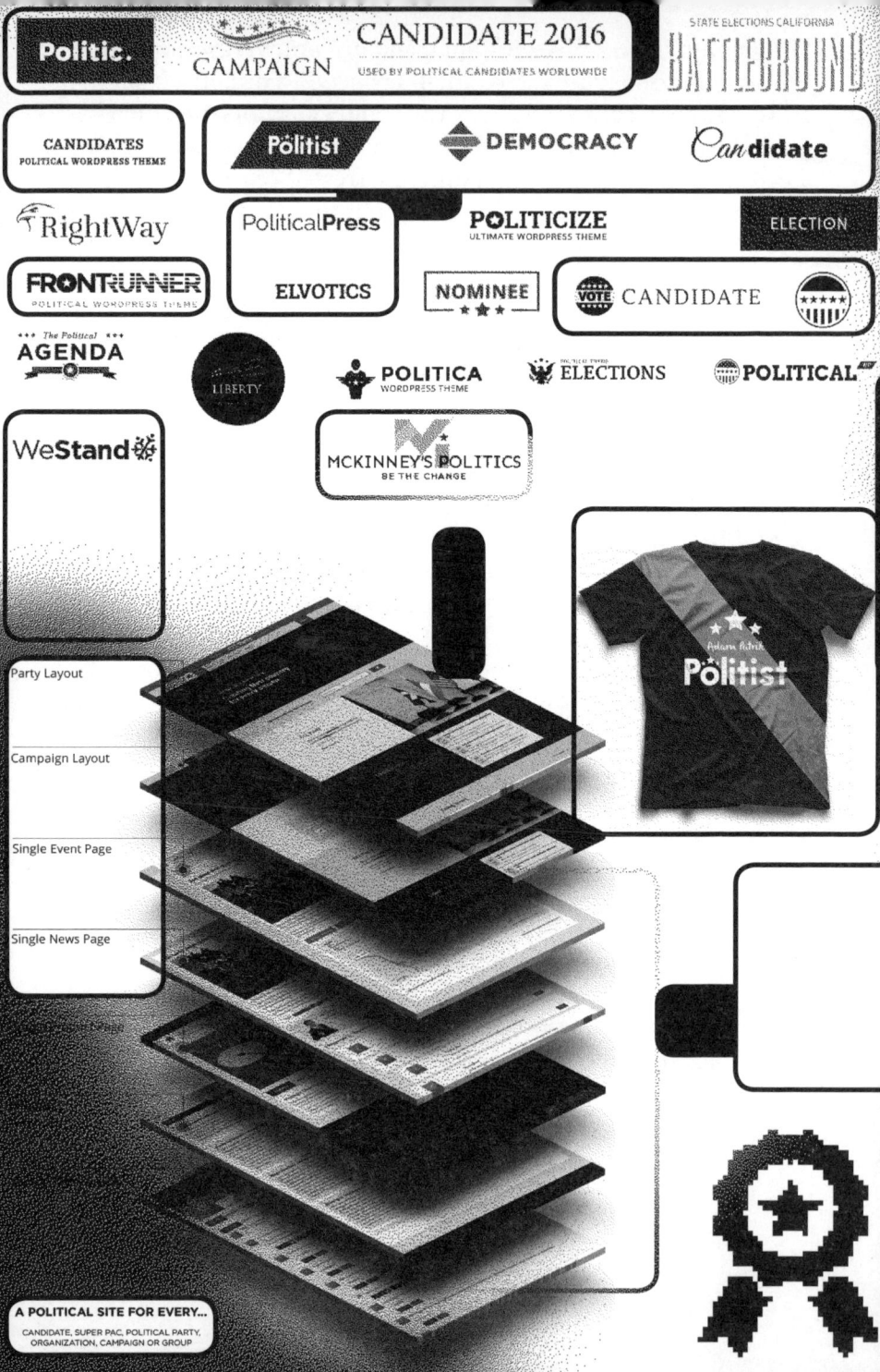

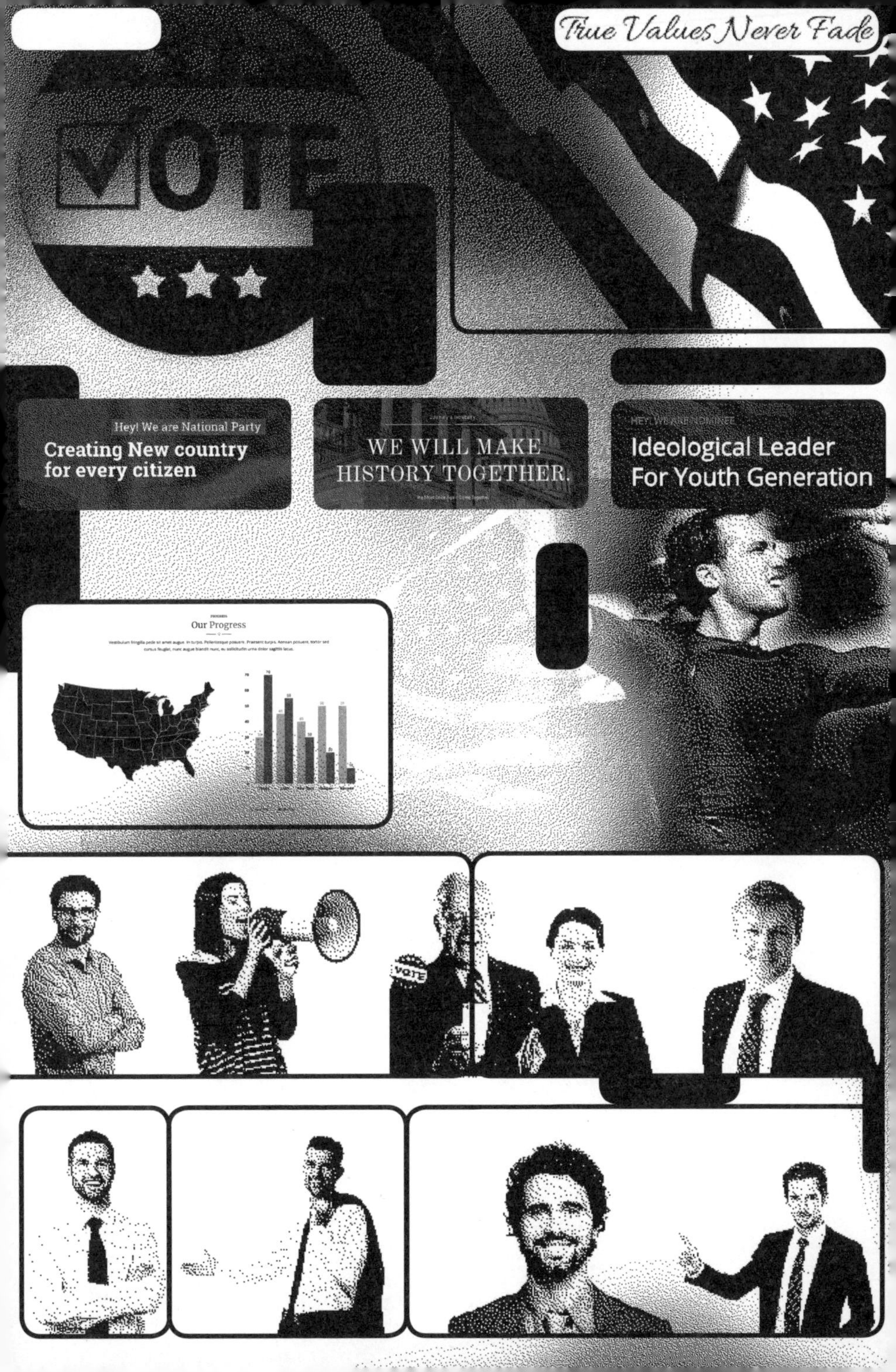

True Values Never Fade

Hey! We are National Party
Creating New country for every citizen

WE WILL MAKE HISTORY TOGETHER.

HEY! WE ARE NOMINEE
Ideological Leader For Youth Generation

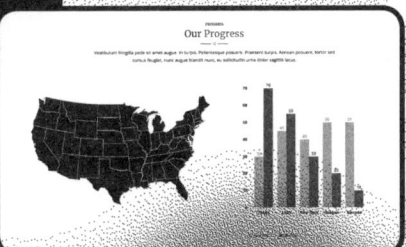
Our Progress

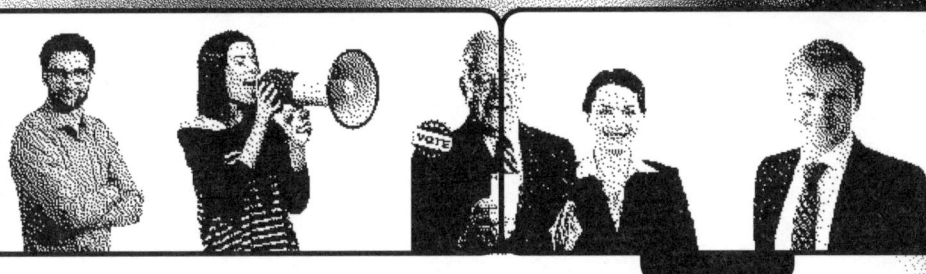

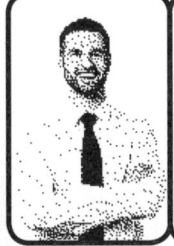

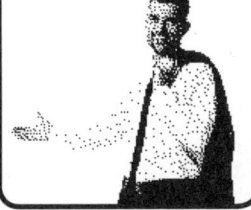

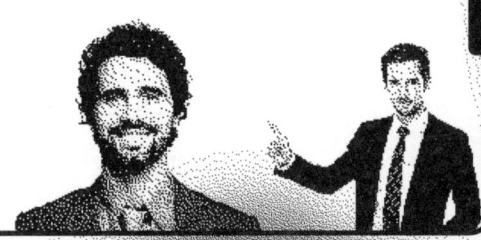

1 CMS: Content Management System, software for editors to publish and edit content online.

2 "Campaign," tbdemos.org, http://tbdemos.org/?theme=Campaign (accessed March 18, 2018).

3 In the past, animations were made with *Adobe Flash* as rendered films that could interact with users' input. Nowadays, code libraries like *jQuery* made it possible to create animations and interactions that are directly connected to live data and are rendered inside the web-browser. But in these cheap political templates, they are just symbols for the *contemporary* web design, without any deeper technical functionalities.

4 Klaus Schmidt, "Identifikation durch Partizipation," *Frankfurter Allgemeine Zeitung*, January 5, 2004.

5 Custom websites, built from the ground up, would cost approximately $5,000 or more.

Imagining Terror:
Propaganda Art Today

Jonas Staal

1   War on Terror Propaganda

The now seventeen-year-old War on Terror has impacted our present global condition in an unprecedented way. This is in part the result of what I call the "expanded state": the merger of public and private infrastructures, state agencies and corporate organizations that operate largely outside of democratic control.[1]

The expanded state has allowed for private military corporations to influence public foreign policy. It has allowed for a new model of war prisons to emerge—such as Guantánamo Bay—in which the rule of law has been replaced by a paranoid military order. It has even allowed for what Jeremy Scahill and Glenn Greenwald have termed "death by metadata": the possibility of being killed through a drone strike simply because one's phone or internet use indicates that one might be indirectly related to a terrorist suspect.[2]

Terror, I argue, begins the moment systems of governmentality move into a realm beyond checks and balances, beyond any form of legal or democratic control. This is the "terror" of the War on Terror. Why did the War on Terror succeed in gaining such enormous political, economic, and judicial power over our lives? When did it claim this power, or when did we as citizens simply hand it over?

In his book *Theater of Operations*, anthropologist and social scientist Joseph Masco claims that to understand the War on Terror we have to look into the heritage of the Cold War, of which he writes the following:

> In the White House, nuclear fear was immediately understood to be not only the basis of American military power, but also a means of installing a new normative reality in the United States, one that could consolidate political power at the federal level by reaching into the internal lives of citizens. […] By focusing Americans on an imminent end of the nation-state, federal authorities mobilized the bomb to create the Cold War consensus of anticommunism, capitalism, and military expansion.³

Masco emphasizes the importance of fear on a collective, nationwide scale. Fear has a political and affective capacity, as it allows regimes of power to forge the idea of a community or nation united in the face of a common threat, across radically different groups and classes. Fear is also what brings us to hand over our agency as citizens to our government: the perpetual image of imminent self-destruction of our families, friends, and communities by a nuclear threat or terrorist agent that paralyzes our capacity for critical examination. It provokes the feeling that we must act instantly, without identifying who exactly we are fighting against, or who exactly we are fighting for.

Inducing this culture of fear is crucial in the construction of a new normative reality in which citizens accept the workings of their government against a supposed enemy without question. This process is essentially what political theorist Noam Chomsky and media theorist Edward Herman defined in the late eighties as the workings of modern propaganda, which deploys fictional threats to increase monopolies of power in the realm of the state and corporate organizations.⁴ Essentially, we accept that we are *no longer citizens*, but instead we become a form of "civil defense" vis-à-vis imagined threats, first in the Cold War, and now in the War on Terror, for the benefit of the shareholders of fear and war. Yet a war to fight fictionalized enemies, once the West's supposed allies such as the regime of Saddam Hussein or the Taliban, has resulted in actual enemies in the franchises of al-Qaeda and the Islamic State.

2   War on Terror Propaganda Art

For a fictional threat to become reality, we have to imagine this threat and visualize it to the point where it becomes an actual reality. Art and culture are crucial means to make a fictionalized war a real one. Film, of course, has always been an essential medium in this regard. In the context of Cold War cinema, we can think of animated films such as *Duck and Cover* (1951) or the televised *The Day After* (1983). Through Cold War cinema, citizens were asked to witness their own destruction, as well as the imminent destruction of the American dream—their consumer utopia and the social order it represented. It is not irrelevant that at the moment of attack in such films women tend to be performing care labor, while men are always laboring for the economic well-being of their families. Yet the image of destruction was also intended to reinforce order at the very same time: this is how life should be.

Film and television have been crucial artistic means to inscribe the image of imminent threat, and cultivate the continuous anxiety and instability that make us willing to voluntarily hand over our political agency to a ruling order. Eyewitnesses to the attacks of September 11 on the Twin Towers experienced immense and devastating shock; witnesses from afar experienced the same horror repeated on screens, with a strange sense of it all having happened before. Had we not already experienced the high-resolution cinematic collapse of our political order in the form of comets in *Armageddon* and *Deep Impact* (1998), Soviet nuclear attacks, aliens, volcanoes, and tidal waves? The conflict experienced by the television audience was that the imagined attack had in a way already superseded the actual attack: real life terrorism was a mere footnote to the countless hours of cinematic destruction that had been internalized already.[5]

Rather than decreasing the level of cinematic apocalypse after September 11, the representation of our own destruction has only expanded to a planetary scale. September 11 was child's play compared to the high-resolution disaster cinema in the form of Roland Emmerich's *2012* (2009) or Zack Snyder's Superman film *Man of Steel* (2013)—the latter of which was subsidized with military materials through the Pentagon Liaison Film Office in Los

Angeles. In contrast, pre-September 11 disaster cinema like *Deep Impact* and *Armageddon* already seem like the new normal.[6]

War on Terror Propaganda Art thus serves to normalize the War on Terror itself. Compared to the planetary state of exception displayed in spectacular disaster cinema, the War on Terror itself seems like a rather modest, contained, and even rational endeavor. Yet there is also a long history of theater and performance wherein citizens not only watch their own destruction but rehearse it, in preparation to become the frontline of civil defense.

Think of the Cold War mass rehearsals of fictional nuclear detonations, evacuations of cities, and so-called duck-and-cover drills, such as the 1955 state-engineered scenario called "Operation Alert." This nation-wide exercise involved a scenario in which sixty cities were hit by a variety of atomic and hydrogen bombs, resulting in over eight million instant deaths and another eight million radiation victims. "Operation Alert" went much further than progressive playwrights and directors like Antonin Artaud, Bertolt Brecht, or Augusto Boal, whose works challenged the relationship of actor and spectator. It turned sixty cities into a theater stage, and turned all of its citizens into actors, and it went beyond questioning the staged nature of reality to create a whole new one through spectacular mass theater.

War on Terror Propaganda Art has continued to develop and perfect the strategies in which citizens perform their own destruction and survival. We can think of the contemporary, biennial state-engineered mass theatrical spectacles known as TOPOFF (Top Officials), consisting of fictional attack scenarios involving supposed weapons of mass destruction used by terrorist agents. The TOPOFF 2 spectacle that took place in 2003 for example, involved eight thousand participants in Seattle and Chicago.[7]

Theater theorist Michelle Dent observed the TOPOFF2 spectacle first hand, and asked herself who exactly was the audience in this bizarre spectacular theater—"the virtual citizens of Seattle? The government officials in-play? The real-time media? The would-be terrorists?"[8]

The answer seems to be all of them, at the same time—yet not just as spectators, but simultaneously as actors. They are, as Boal termed it, "spect-actors," establishing the new realities of the War of Terror by collectively performing their destruction from it.⁹

The new normal is constructed through continuous threat production: War on Terror Propaganda Art gives visual form to these threats. What we perform, when we are engaged in War on Terror Propaganda Art through its cinema or theater, is to become "Us," in the "Us/Them" dichotomy that lies at the ideological foundation of the War on Terror.

The paradoxical reality of our time is that we are actually faced with real threats, in the form of massive economic deprivation and inequality, diminishments of civil rights and democratic control, structural racism and violent exclusion, and the planetary danger of climate change. War on Terror Propaganda Art forces us to forget these actual existential threats by turning our attention to an imagined imminent threat.

3   Stephen K. Bannon: A Case-Study

Separating propaganda art into different disciplines—into separate domains of film or theater—in fact counteracts its interdisciplinary essence: propaganda art aims to be everywhere, through every possible means of mediation. Constructing a new normative reality demands repetition through all possible channels, without interruption or hesitation.

In that context, we turn to a contemporary propaganda artist who connects art with cinema, popular culture, media, politics, and activism: Stephen K. Bannon. His career spans widely different fields of interest: after climbing ranks in the United States Navy, Bannon joined the investment bank Goldman Sachs, before becoming editor of Breitbart News.

Since its founding in 2007, Breitbart has become the self-proclaimed platform of the "alternative right" or "alt-right" in short, although writer Angela Nagle argues that it fits better to the European-nationalist styled agenda of the "alt-light."¹⁰ It has since mobilized millions of readers through aggressive articles aimed against progressives and left politics, immigrants, refugees, the LGBTQI+ community, and feminists. It was Bannon's success at Breitbart that brought him to the head of Trump's presidential campaign and later as the Chief White House Strategist for the first year of Trump's presidency. Although Bannon was forced out of the White House for his links to the alt-right, and later stepped down as editor of Breitbart due to the publication of Michael Wolff's *Fire and Fury*, his organizational influence on the international alt-right remains significant. This includes, for example, a recent European tour of talks and lectures for the Italian League, the French Front National, and the German Alternative for Germany.[11]

It is lesser known that Bannon is also a prolific film-maker. He began as a producer of Hollywood films in the 1990s, such as Sean Penn's *The Indian Runner* (1991), and *Titus* (1999) featuring Anthony Hopkins. In between, he headed the Biosphere 2 Earth system science research facility in Oracle, Arizona from 1993 to 1995 (the "first" Biosphere being planet Earth itself): the largest closed ecological system ever created, where he researched the consequences of climate change. In the late '90s he wrote a "rap-musical" with script writer Julia Jones entitled *The Thing I Am*, an interpretation of Shakespeare's last work set in the context of the Rodney King riots in South Central Los Angeles.[12]

Although his work with Biosphere 2 shows Bannon's interests in engineering social environments, and his "rap-musical" displays particular clichés of black culture, one could generally say that in this period he was still influenced by a rather liberal-progressive Hollywood environment.[13] That all changed after September 11, when Bannon began transforming into one of the most influential propagandist and propaganda artists of our time. From then onward, he began to develop his own particular brand of documentary-film pamphlets, of which he would make ten in total from 2004 until 2018.

Bannon's first film is a biopic titled *In the Face of Evil: Reagan's War in Word and Deed* (2004). The film presents a glorified life story of the Republican president, portraying Reagan as a lone but dedicated hero facing the evil of the Soviet Union. In the final part of the film, the attacks on the Twin Towers are shown, emphasizing Bannon's view that yet again, Western civilization faces an existential threat. This time it's not Cold War Communism, but War on Terror Islamism. Bannon's message was clear: a new

Reagan is needed to wage an unapologetic war in the face of the cyclical return of evil.

Like Bannon's obsession with strong leadership, fringe conspiracy sciences mark another characteristic of his work. *The Fourth Turning*, a book by William Strauss and Neil Howe from 1997, argues that civilizations develop through four cycles: from their rise to greatness to their decline and downfall.[14] Bannon, relying heavily on this text in his work, belies a paradoxical view of how "greatness" is defined. He is a free market conservative-Christian who has called for the "destruction of the administrative state."[15] Yet he promotes "economic nationalism" in which a government is responsible to maintain the free market within its national borders, protected by a strong military and massive border control resulting in what we could call "white Christian economic nationalism."[16]

The Fourth Turning was the starting point of Bannon's film *Generation Zero* (2010), which outlines a deterministic view of history. In his perception, the United States gained greatness after the Second World War through a home-grown free capitalist market, strong religious and family values, military might, and a proud national identity. In the post-war generation, however, the Flower Power and feminist movements introduced secular and individualist consumer culture that would bring about the degradation of the US by establishing the rule of a liberal globalist elite, or what Bannon has called the "Party of Davos," referencing the yearly gathering of CEO's in the World Economic Forum in Davos, Switzerland. To Bannon, there is a direct lineage from the social movements of the '60s and '70s to the hedonist and individualist culture that led to the 2008 economic crisis, essentially one of liberal-globalist greed. This decline announces the "fourth turning," a great war between his ideal of white Christian economic nationalism against the internal enemy in the form of the Party of Davos, and an external enemy in the form of Islamic terrorism.

Formally, Bannon's work follows clear documentary stylistic conventions. Voiceovers of frequently unnamed "experts" lead us through what look like historical documents that are to provide proof to his argument of a cyclical rise and fall of civilizations. This narrative is strengthened by less informative footage, such as ticking clocks, rotting fruit, blazing tanks, and guns, all of which affirm a sense of inevitability. Bannon's narrative cannot be paused or reversed, but races from one cycle to the next. Arousing music underscores each of these phases, adding an emotional and affective dimension to the viewer witnessing the rise and fall of its own society. The viewer is made to feel powerless and alone: repetitive cycles cannot be reversed or stopped, we are passive witnesses to our own rise and fall without control over our destiny.

Regarding his inspirations, Bannon has said: "I'm a student of Michael Moore's films, of Eisenstein, Riefenstahl. Leave the politics aside, you have to learn from those past masters on how they were trying to communicate their ideas."[17] It is a rather ambitious statement: Bannon's fast-produced films, full of stock footage, lack the originality of Moore or the artistic innovation of Eisenstein or Riefenstahl—but that does not mean that they're not effective. He has termed his style "Kinetic Cinema," characterized by situating repeated narratives closely to a bombardment of images to the point at which, in his own words, it "almost overwhelms the audience."[18] At such a peak moment of induced anxiety and fear, Bannon's answer is introduced. In his first film the answer was Reagan, who faces up to the threat of communism; the intention of his subsequent films is to seek for the Reagan of the 21st century who stands up against the two-headed enemy of the Party of Davos and Islamic terrorism. As Bannon has put it: "What I've tried to do is weaponize film."[19]

In *The Undefeated* (2011), Bannon portrays former vice-presidential candidate Sarah Palin as his champion. Combined with images of Reagan, Palin is depicted as a people's hero: an icon of the free west, a fighter for economic nationalism, and simultaneously a dedicated mother who upholds the values of family and defends Christian doctrine. Liberal-democratic leaders such as Barack Obama are, on the other hand, portrayed in his film *The Hope & The Change* (2012) as symptoms of a degenerate secular and individualist culture of appeasement. Bannon also sees a direct link between the Obama administration and the Occupy movement, which he considers a staged protest orchestrated by Obama administrators, labor unions, and the hackers collective Anonymous. In the narration of his film *Occupy Unmasked* (2012), the globalist elites (represented by Obama) and the radical-left, or "alt-left" (represented by Occupy), are both part of a "cultural Marxist" coup, aimed to take-over and collectivize the state from within.[20] Obama and Occupy are the threats within, Islamic fundamentalism is the threat outside. A strong leader is needed to defeat both.

Torchbearer (2016), Bannon's paranoid and apocalyptic view of a Western civilization on the brink of collapse, takes the most extreme stance. It is also his most explicitly religious film: only the return to the Christian, nationalist, and free-market ideal of American society—the majestic "first turning"—provides a solution to inevitable apocalypse. Narrated by arch-conservative figurehead Phil Robertson, a prominent anti-gay, anti-feminist, and anti-abortion activist known from the reality television show *Duck Dynasty*, Bannon does more than simply overpower us with images of violence, chaos, and decadence: he provides us a way out, exemplified by the final scenes in which Robertson baptizes what seem to be the viewers of the very same film. In the peace and quiet of rural America, they are inaugurated by their religious leader into the civil defense of Bannon's white Christian economic nationalism.

Torchbearer came out the year Bannon joined the Trump campaign. It might be hard to imagine Trump as the symbol of white Christian economic nationalism, considering his sexism, playboy persona, and multiple marriages, previous financial support to democrats, and his continued use of government aid for his failing casinos and real estate ventures. Bannon's campaign, however, secured the support of evangelicals and Christian communities who helped bring Trump to power. Bannon scripted and staged Trump according to how his constituents desired to see him. What Bannon failed to do with Palin, he did with Trump: he made his own Reagan.

Throughout his body of film works, one can easily recognize Bannon's core narratives and strategies. His "kinetic" cinema became a kinetic political campaign, twisting and manipulating reality to the point where only a Trump could save us. Whether allegations of sexism, racism, or other controversy, Bannon staged and reimaged reality to make Trump. This is the power of War on Terror Propaganda Art, or, in the case of Steve Bannon, something between War on Terror Propaganda Art and the Propaganda Art of the Alternative-Right.[21] After having cultivated the narrative of a new clash of civilizations through his work for nearly fifteen years, Bannon turned artistic imaginary into a political reality.

To artists and cultural workers, the present task is to research and understand the processes in which propaganda and propaganda art construct our current reality. Propaganda is, in essence, the performance of power, the employment of various infrastructures—in the realms of politics, the economy, media, and the military—to construct a new normative reality.[22] Considering that there is no reality absent from power, one has to question whether there is ever a politics without propaganda. But not all powers are alike, and thus *propagandas* in the plural might differ and conflict as well. The powers of the War on Terror and Bannon's international alt-right are fundamentally different than those of popular mass movements, from Occupy to Black Lives Matter, pan-European platforms such as DiEM25, or the stateless democracy of the Rojava Revolution in northern Syria. They might not be able to avoid performing a propaganda of their own, but theirs is one that proposes an egalitarian narrative about the reality we live in and the world we can create collectively.[23]

As artists and cultural workers, our endeavor should be to introduce new narratives about where we come from, who we are, and most of all who we can still become—not simply in the form of a counter-propaganda, but by exploring the possibility of an emancipatory propaganda art.

This essay was presented in an earlier form as two lectures: the first titled "Art against the War on Terror" during the conference Public Calling, on November 1, 2016, at the National Theatre in Oslo organized by Fritt Ord Foundation and KORO—Public Art Norway / URO; the second titled "Imagining Terror: Propaganda Art Today," on November 30, 2017, at Het Nieuwe Instituut, Rotterdam.

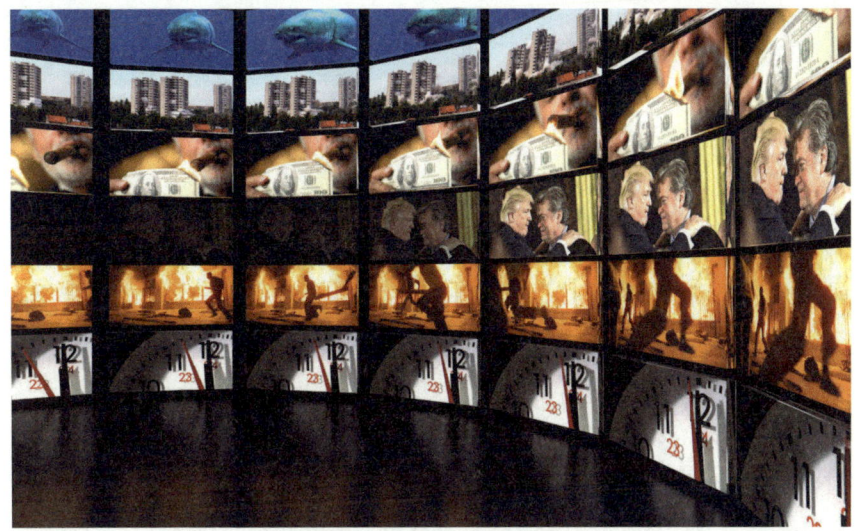

Jonas Staal, *Steve Bannon: A Propaganda Retrospective*, 2018
Produced by Het Nieuwe Instituut, Rotterdam
Stills from Steve Bannon's film *Generation Zero* (2010)
Image: Remco van Bladel and Jonas Staal

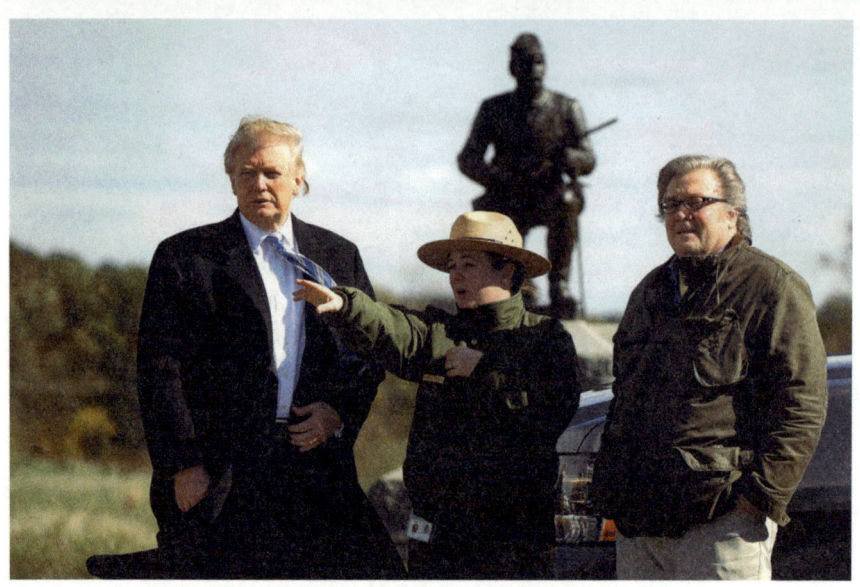

Jonas Staal, *The Disappearance of Steve Bannon*, 2018
Produced by Het Nieuwe Instituut, Rotterdam

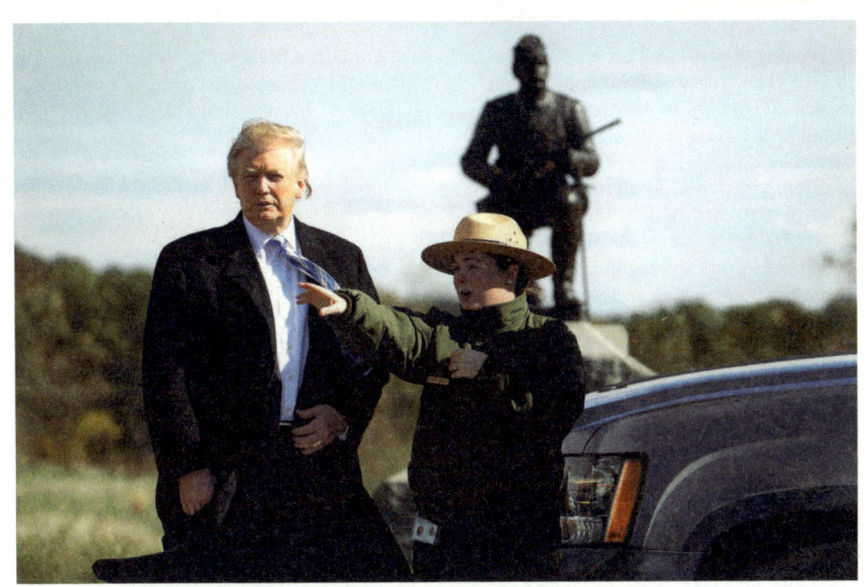

Jonas Staal

1
According to artist and geographer Trevor Paglen, the complexity of mapping the expanded state in the War on Terror is because its infrastructures are by definition conceived as a "secret geography," one that is not merely hidden by the state, but "designed to exist outside the law." Trevor Paglen, *Blank Spots on the Map: The Dark Geography of the Pentagon's Secret World* (London: New American Library, 2010), 140.

2
Jeremy Scahill and Glenn Greenwald, "The NSA's Secret Role in the U.S. Assassination Program," *The Intercept*, February 10, 2014, online at: https://firstlook.org/theintercept/article/2014/02/10/the-nsas-secret-role/.

3
Joseph Masco, *The Theater of Operations* (Durham, NC: Duke University Press, 2014), 48. The impact on the physical, psychological, political, economic, technological, ecological, and finally geographic landscapes of the Cold War are discussed in detail in Masco's *The Nuclear Borderlands: The Manhattan Project in Post-Cold War New Mexico* (Princeton: Princeton University Press, 2006).

4
Noam Chomsky and Edward S. Herman, *Manufacturing Consent: The Political Economy of the Mass Media* (New York: Pantheon Books, 1988).

5
For a further analysis of the intersection between imagined and material terror, see: Terence McSweeney, *The "War on Terror" and American Film: 9/11 Frames Per Second* (Edinburgh: Edinburgh University Press, 2016).

6
On the work of the Pentagon Liaison Film Office, see: David L. Robb, *Operation Hollywood: How the Pentagon Shapes and Censors the Movies* (Amherst: Prometheus Books, 2004).

7
US Department of State, "Top Officials" (TOPOFF) information page, http://2001-2009.state.gov/s/ct/about/c16661.htm.

8
Michelle Dent, "Staging Disaster: Reporting Live (Sort of) from Seattle," *The Drama Review* 48, no. 4 (Winter 2004): 109–34.

9
The concept of "spect-actor" is theorized by Boal as part of his famous concept of the *Theater of the Oppressed* (1974). The central idea is that participants stage their own external and internalized conditions of oppression, acting out their oppression, while being spectators to it at the same time. As Boal writes: "The members of the audience must become the Character: possess him, take his place—not obey him, but guide him, show him the path they think right. In this way the Spectator becoming Spect-Actor is democratically opposed to the other members of the audience, free to invade the scene and appropriate the power of the actor." Boal thus proposes his methodology as a transgressive theater practice, which, in the context of War on Terror Propaganda is radically perverted. Here spect-actors are supposed to enact a disaster and witness its impact to transpose their agency to that of the expanded state, rather than to claim this agency themselves. See Augusto Boal, *Theater of the Oppressed* (London: Pluto Press, 2008), xxi.

10
Angela Nagle, *Kill All Normies: Online Culture Wars from 4Chan and Tumblr to Trump and the Alt-Right* (Winchester, UK: Zero Books, 2017).

11
According to Joshua Green, this recent tour is the product of a long term international alt-right network build by Bannon, that reaches from "Nigel Farage and UKIP, Marine Le Pen's National Front, Geert Wilders and the Party for Freedom, and Sarah Palin and the Tea Party." Joshua Green, *Devil's Bargain: Steve Bannon, Donald Trump, and the Storming of the Presidency* (New York: Penguin Books, 2017), 207.

12
A table read of the script was presented as an online televised performance by *Nowthis News* in 2016, see: https://nowthisnews.com/steve-bannon-hip-hop-rap-musical.

13
The Washington Post notes in this regard: "'The Thing I Am' presents Los Angeles during the riots as a war zone equivalent to the one created by the clash between the Romans and the Volscians. And Coriolanus' rise and downfall in 'The Thing I Am' present him as someone who could stop the violence in his own community but is temperamentally incapable of making the compromises and taking the strong stands necessary to do so. These ideas have a striking resonance with the ways President Trump now talks about American cities and African American communities." Alyssa Rosenberg, "Stephen Bannon Wrote a Movie about the 1992 L.A. Riots. Now, You Can Finally Watch It," *Washington Post*, May 1, 2017.

14
In Strauss and Howe's own words: "Turnings come in cycles of four. Each spans the length of a long human life, roughly eighty to a hundred years, a unit of time the ancient called the *saeculum*. Together, the four turnings of the saeculum comprise history's seasonal rhythm of growth, maturation, entropy, and destruction." William Strauss and Neil Howe, *The Fourth Turning: An American Prophecy* (New York: Broadway Books, 1997), 3.

15
Max Fisher, "Stephen K. Bannon's CPAC Comments, Annotated and Explained," *New York Times*, February 24, 2017.

16
Fisher.

17
Adam Wren, "What I Learned Binge-Watching Steve Bannon's Documentaries," *POLITICO*, December 2, 2016.

18
John Patterson, "For Haters Only: Watching Steve Bannon's Documentary Films," *Guardian*, November 29, 2016.

19
Keith Koffler, *Bannon: Always the Rebel* (Washington, DC: Regnery Publishing, 2017), 48.

20
The term "cultural Marxism" originally related to a model of cultural critique of mass standardization and commodification developed in the context of the philosophy and sociology of the Frankfurt School. In movements assembled under Trumpism the term has come to signify a conspiracy theory that claims that the radical left, or sometimes a left-Jewish alliance, is using popular culture to plan a government takeover. The main target is the Jewish-American writer and community organizer Saul Alinsky (1909–72) and his book *Rules for Radicals* (1971). Both the Clintons, Obama and the Occupy movement are considered by Bannon and other right-wing ideologies to operate under the continuous influence of Alinksy ideology.

21
Journalist David Neiwert's detailed reconstruction of converging right-wing extremist movements past and present—from the Patriot militia to the Tea Party and alt-right, resulting in the construction of an "alt-America," comes very close to the alt-right propaganda objective to create a new, parallel reality all together. See: David Neiwert, *Alt-America: The Rise of the Radical Right in the Age of Trump* (New York: Verso, 2017).

22
This definition follows the work of Chomsky and Herman referenced earlier, who speak of the "performance" of the mass media in contributing to a new normative reality that follows the interests over their ownership. Different than Chomsky and Herman though, in the context of contemporary propaganda *art*, I propose to read the term performance both as a formal analysis of the "enactment" of power, but also of the theatrical means necessary to script choreograph and "stage" reality. I further propose a propaganda model that does not exclude progressive and emancipatory forms of emerging power—different than Chomsky and Herman's sole focus on "monopolized" power—to analyze possible alternative forms of "emancipatory propaganda" in popular mass movements, stateless insurgencies and the like.

23
See also, Jonas Staal, "Assemblism," *e-flux journal*, no. 80, March 2017.

Negative Internationalism and Shame as Strategy
Nina Power

How do we conceive of our humanity today? Are "we" post-human (or are "some" of "us"? The problem of the "we" is the question here), living out our lives in indifference to what unifies us as a species, wondering if we have been rendered different by technology, or by capitalism, or by geography? Is the new global divide not between north and south, rich and poor, imperium and periphery, bourgeoisie and proletariat, but rather between those who have transcended humanity (whether through the satiation of want, technology, or fantasy, apathy, indifference) and those who are forced to remain resolutely trapped inside its definition? What do I mean by humanity here? I am not necessarily or directly referring to the biological substrate that unites us, though that is one way of conceiving the shared nature of humanity at the level of species. Nor am I appealing to a putative set of "rights" that some possess and others do not, but that in principle should be universal (though again, this is a possible political avenue, and one with some limited success historically).

Despite all the conceptual ways in which we might imagine that humanity can be conceived in a global sense—the pictures of Earth from space or the "globalization" of capitalism, the implication of which is that we might also be able to imagine a "global humanity"—we are no closer to overcoming the fictions of nations, race, or of defeating fascisms of all kinds. In fact, we are barely able to rise above the creeping, individualizing feeling that "everything is wrong."

Neoliberal individualism has morphed into a terrifying collective suspicion, what Thomas Curran and Andrew Hill call "socially prescribed perfectionism":

> The feeling of paranoia and anxiety engendered by the persistent—and not entirely unfounded—sensation that everyone is waiting for you to make a mistake so they can write you off forever. This hyper-perception of others' impossible expectations causes social alienation, neurotic self-examination, feelings of shame and unworthiness.[1]

Post and trans-humanist fantasies, and the desire that cyberspace will unleash limitless human freedoms, appear to be snagged on that most human of feelings: *shame*. This is not the shame that Marx thought might already be a kind of "revolution," the shame that comes from a collective attempt to face up to what might be wrong, together, the kind that coils like a lion about to pounce, but rather the sort of shame Freud identified with femininity in 1933: "The suppression of women's aggressiveness which is prescribed for them constitutionally and imposed upon them socially favours the development of powerful masochistic impulses, which succeed, as we know, in binding erotically the destructive trends which have been diverted inwards."[2]

There is no doubt that we are drowning in anxiety. We struggle to think of ourselves collectively, and we spend much of our time trying to cope with "a sense of self overwhelmed by pathological worry and a fear of negative social evaluation, characterized by a focus on deficiencies, and sensitive to criticism and failure," as Curran and Hill put it.[3]

Can we turn shame around? The opposite of shame, we might reasonably say, is pride: a mobilizing force in the struggle for civil rights, particularly racial and sexual equality. Today pride is sneaked away ever-more by the right—pride in "one's country," in "one's race," in "one's sex"—masculinity (and misogyny), nationalism and racial supremacy walk hand in hand. If it is difficult to reclaim pride for the left, can we perhaps embrace certain forms of lack, or weakness? We are accustomed to regarding weakness *as* weak, which is to say, to value it negatively. But what might we able to do with a weak resistance? Philosopher Ewa Majewska suggests that:

[The] logic of the political agency of the weak is what makes it possible to understand today's excluded as those who, even if they "cannot speak," can have an impact on the political, sometimes even changing it without planning to. This scenario—a new beginning from a place of fear and uncertainty—is similar to the conditions for the appearance of a territory as described by Deleuze and Guattari in *Anti-Oedipus*. Importantly, the core of artistic creativity is found in the same place: a place of fear and weakness, not of power. The political agency of the weak—*weak resistance*—is therefore much more appropriate than traditional forms of resistance for discussing artistic responses to the micro-fascist takeover of desires and souls.[4]

Fascism in all its iterations celebrates masculinity, strength, dominance and abhors women and any other group—homosexuals, minorities, disabled people—that do not possess power. Is there anything new in today's fascist revival? Yes, and no. What remains is the fetishization and desire for power and domination. As Majewska puts it:

> What is new in contemporary fascism? It seems that fascist agents are not entirely fixated on the state and its institutions. It is not a top-down movement. It is a kind of right-wing insurgency, organized from below. This molecular movement rewires fascism's former articulations, in which hierarchical forms of organization played a major role. Obviously, the state remains the central stake in fascists' drive to power. However, the Polish version of homemade fascism started long before the Law and Justice Party took over power. Nascent state-fascism is aligned with fascisms-from-below, or with what Deleuze and Guattari called micro-fascisms.[5]

We can see how this pincer-movement, how the state and the insurgency, increasingly come together in various parts of Europe, such as Poland. We can also see how a certain kind of irreverent, "subversive," violent, ironic style has become the preserve of the alt-right online and then what this looks like on the streets—in Charlottesville in the US, in Macerata in Italy, on borders everywhere—and in politics, in figures such as Marine Le Pen, Norbert Hofer, Frauke Petry. The fascisms-from-below meet the fascisms-from above, and those that have always been "othered" are othered yet further, in increasingly violent ways. The way in which capitalism intersects with fascism is a complicated one, and I will not discuss it here, except to say (with Walter Benjamin) that whoever is not willing to talk about capitalism should also keep quiet about fascism. We cannot analyze the state of contemporary fascism without also talking about the market, and about the way in which capitalism divides us from each other, pillages the earth, and creates devastation on an untold scale.

Fascism will use the tactics and allure of victimhood to convince its adherents that they are under attack—from migrants, from refugees, from people of color, from women—and we must be careful that any attempt to identify a collective weakness, shame or lack does not fall into the fascist trap of filling in that lack with an enemy who is to blame. The kind of lack I want to defend here as the basis for an internationalism is a constitutively human one, an existential condition and not an "emptiness" suffered only by a few and "filled" with fables and false narratives.

So, what is this thing, "negative internationalism," this type of solidarity that takes seriously the condition of shame and weak resistance? It is the recognition that we are all vulnerable, but that some of us are currently more vulnerable than others, and that others are in position to help protect those who need the means of survival. It is a kind of humanism based not on what we share, but what we could all potentially lack—the means of survival. It begins from the assumption of vulnerability and of the dependency of us all on each other. If capitalism renders us incapable of seeing the human relations behind commodities while fascism constructs directed hate based on lies, negative internationalism instead puts us directly in mind of our shared humanity, despite everything that threatens to make us see only differences.

1
Meagan Day, "Under Neoliberalism, You Can Be Your Own Tyrannical Boss," Jacobinmag.com, https://www.jacobinmag.com/2018/01/under-neoliberalism-you-can-be-your-own-tyrannical-boss (accessed December 1, 2018).

2
Sigmund Freud, "New Introductory Lecturer on Psycho-Analysis, Lecture 33, Femininity," *The Essentials of Psycho-Analysis*, trans. James Strachey (London: Vintage Books, 2005), 415.

3
Day, "Under Neoliberalism, You Can Be Your Own Tyrannical Boss."

4–5
Ewa Majewska and Kuba Szreder. "So Far, So Good: Contemporary Fascism, Weak Resistance, and Postartistic Practices in Today's Poland," *e-flux journal*, no.76 (2018), https://www.e-flux.com/journal/76/71467/so-far-so-good-contemporary-fascism-weak-resistance-and-postartistic-practices-in-today-s-poland/ (accessed December 1, 2018).

Solidarity without Sameness
Patricia Reed

The question of what it means to be human, of what humanity means today, has resurged in the wake of the Anthropocene — that geological epoch unleashed by human hands and where we humans have subsequently entered into a broadened "we," as collective subjects of natural history.[1] This plight simultaneously points to our dominance over the world, while humbly flattening us into common species-creatures with other life-forms, endangered by our own force in a state of potent impotency. Additionally, and partly conjoined with the Anthropocene, techno-computational developments have begun to transform our bio-physiological limits, and further stand to burst the contours of anthropomorphic intelligence we once figured as being our exclusive defining quality. Combined, it seems we may be living in the prehistory of something radically other, where human self-understanding is unstable, undergoing revision, and a new, unknown world is on the cusp of becoming reality.[2] The range of theoretical and practical responses to this condition are as polarized as a twitter war, from those who blindly champion overcoming the human in favor of machinic "perfection" whatever the cost, to those who lament the loss of our "essential humanity," where our atrocities suddenly become erased from memory. Wherever one situates themselves along this spectrum, these turbulences, uncertainties, and sets of risks that cascade from them, as such, are indisputable. What is and must be entirely contestable is *how* we will navigate them, but that question of how, in the very least, entails a negotiation, understanding and an adjudication of them. This generic human existential crisis, like all crises, is both a promise and a threat. Ignoring these conditions as if they do not exist is by far the greatest risk, especially since these transformations play out at a planetary scale.

Despite the long-standing ambitions to conceive of humanity from an expansive proportion, the scale of the shared crises we face render these generically existential questions urgently necessary—not only philosophically, but ethically and pragmatically as well. What sorts of concepts can we develop to fathom "humanity," and how can we learn to *exist in* those very concepts? This latter point of *existing in* concepts is essential. It is one thing to say that all humans belong to the "we" of geohistory, for example, but it is quite another to transform this saying into behavioral traction. Countless injustices have been unleashed from this category we call "human," and those traumas don't magically disappear out of historical convenience or our present crises that acutely demand maximal solidarity. Many of said traumas have been enacted in the name of cosmopolitanism, but have been enacted as a brutally bloated Eurocentric particularity thrust onto the world to dominate and conform humanity into a homogenous mold of itself—that is, into a familiar image. Until the historical exclusivity of this category "human" is grappled with, hopes that we humans may unite under the common threat of the Anthropocene remain an ahistorical idealism, trapping us in the immobility of wishful thinking. We cannot brush historical reality aside, but we can amend our paths and corresponding epistemologies because of it. Nor can we let that historical reality arrest us absolutely, as we face up to an indispensable project of planetary-scale humanity for our survival and potential flourishing.

A decade ago, at the precipice of the global financial crisis, Mark Fisher reflected on the necessity to construct a collective subject that could measure up to the impersonal, abstract systems that govern our relations with each other and the world, noting the impossibility of substantially transforming our world by reducing these complex, structural dynamics into personalized, moral ones.[3] Such a demand persists as we see the widespread ideological disinvestment in the project of *unilateral* globalization[4] since the 2008 crash, having manifest not in speculative models for progressive coexistence as one may have hoped, but in anachronistic nationalisms on the far right. Despite our profoundly transformed and transforming techno-material condition, the old fictions of the nation have reignited the imaginations of many, as Nina Power has noted.[5] The cooptation of the disaffection for unilateral globalization by the far right, as Power writes, is premised on racist strategies of blame and othering, manipulating the precarious conditions endured by many toward a violently unreal politics that refuses to confront the actual crises and causal forces driving this lived precarity. The far right traffics in frightening images of a simplified world, a world-picture where one is deceptively sold the false option to bunker down in the isolated safety of national familiarity, to the disavowal and conceptual elimination of extra-local, interdependent and complex reality. We ought to recall that such a world-picture serves as the root for all fascisms, namely: a world-picture wherein one imagines one can choose with *whom* one lives.[6] This refusal of difference, communicated through purified world-images, fundamentally rejects the political question of *how* we choose to cohabitate by transposing it with a destructive, reductive imaginary that wills to shove all that is foreign away, as if it did not exist.

The first step for a collective subject, is to resolutely negate the decideability of with whom we live—that is to say, cohabitation is a domain of *unchoosing*.[7] The more arduous next step is to affirm the question of how we coexist in definitively constructive ways. Such a collective subject is one that not only stands against the vicious premise of purification at the heart of the decision "with whom we live," but can also navigate a complex world in-common. In this regard, the collective subject cannot be premised by principles of likeness, by principles of familiarity. It demands, rather, a mode of solidarity without homophily, without sameness. Crucially, this collective subject is affirmatively impure, negotiating its partial complicity within social and economic structures that enable fascist tendencies to arise at all. As Sven Lütticken notes in his statement for the project "Propositions for a Non-Fascist Life," one cannot simply other or externalize fascists absolutely, those profoundly and despicably unlike "us," as if doing so provides inoculation from their infectious hate.[8] Resisting and battling against such tendencies, means there is no opting out, no outright separation to be had on a personal level, so long as those impersonal, systemic enabling conditions of violence and inequality persist. To extrapolate and give specificity to the question Judith Butler posed in her Adorno Prize lecture,[9] is it possible to lead a truly non-fascist life within those very social conditions that enable it? I would simply argue no.

The collective subject overflows the boundaries of our individual skins into the realm of the unfamiliar. In keeping with Fisher, it is a mode of impersonal subjecthood that can labor toward just, often abstract, systemic change untenable through sheer moralism or individual behavior choices. For him, because this subject does not yet exist, it demands construction—it isn't simply given to us, nor is it waiting to be discovered. It needs to be built. It needs libidinal and cognitive investment in *gluing agents* that can urge it into collective materialization. So, how are we to mitigate this seeming contradiction in the formulation above: of requiring a conceptual "glue" to cohere as collective subjects, yet a mode of coherence without the imperatives of familiarity, sameness or homogeneity? Otherwise formulated, can we conceive of a universalism without obliterating difference, and what would it mean to exist in that concept?

With her "negative internationalism," Power provides an important contribution to this dilemma, not by proposing a rallying slogan of common identification, but a "glue" based on our shared human vulnerabilities, and that which we may all (at one point) lack: "the means of survival," noting that this vulnerability is deeply, unevenly distributed.[10] One could easily add other life-forms to this list, since humans are hardly innocent, nor the only vulnerable creatures. Her negative internationalism situates care at the center of a speculative, interdependent ordering, a proposition that antagonizes the winner-take-all ethos of neoliberal individualism, where we have been competitively training for decades under the presumption of atomized independence. As many feminists, Power included, have been rightly arguing for years, care and reproductive labor have always formed a societal backbone, however drastically undervalued. Her negative internationalism remedies that undervaluation by militating for care as the primary assumption from which the nurturing of compassion and noncompetitive relations can be enabled. If capitalism requires the root assumption that we are incentivized only by self-interest and selfishness, how may we start to imagine the structural consequences of assuming care/vulnerability as a base premise through which relations and interactions play out? What kind of world could unfold from those hypothetical assumptions?

With vulnerability defined in terms of a possible lack of "the means of survival," we need to complicate this question further by submitting it to the multi-scalar demands of our time. How are we to account for the "means of survival" at the level of a singular human *and* at the species-level of humanity as such? This multi-scalar criterion for care rests on the fact that care cannot be limited to an intimate scale of interpersonal relations when it concerns life and livability itself for over seven billion of us. Care among humans and nonhumans must extend to the biospheric conditions that sustain us all in the first place, signalling the necessity for "care" to become interwoven with robust epistemological endeavors. As Power has elsewhere suggested, emotionality linked to compassion and reason are "not mortal enemies."[11] We cannot adequately care if we do not possess better accounts of reality[12] that guide us on how to care. We cannot directly care for everyone or everything, but we ought to care they are cared for. This insistence on an expanded picture of care, stands in ethical and epistemological opposition to the logic of the far right, who assert a perilous world-image of isolationism backed by relations of familiarity. It is not only a morally bankrupt world-image, but an epistemologically erroneous one as well, as it refuses to acknowledge the reality of our shared condition in-common. Theirs is, quite falsely, a very small world.

To care in an expanded way, our world-picture needs to be commensurate with the proportions of reality today, which means learning to care for unfamiliar relations and knowing how to care at the scale of the impersonal. Following Power's claim in pointing to a common lack as a glue between humans, so too may we add that the collective subject is ultimately a project for solidarity without sameness.

1
Tristan Garcia, *Nous* (Paris: Éditions Grasset & Fasquelle, 2016), 49. [Available only in French at the time of publishing.]

2
For an elaborate account of the revisioning of human intelligence *qua* computation, see: Reza Negarestani, *Intelligence and Spirit* (Falmouth, UK: Urbanomic × Sequence Press, 2017).

3
Mark Fisher, *Capitalist Realism: Is There No Alternative?* (London: Zero Books, 2009), 66.

4
I take this term of "unilateral globalization" from Yuk Hui wherein he uses it to describe the elevation of regionally-bound Eurocentric / Anglo-Atlantic Alliance particular epistemologies to a global metaphysics. See Yuk Hui, "Cosmotechnics as Cosmopolitics," *e-flux journal*, no. 86 (2017), http://www.e-flux.com/journal/86/161887/cosmotechnics-as-cosmopolitics/.

5
Nina Power, "Negative Internationalism and Shame as Strategy," 155, in this volume.

6
Bonnie Honig, *Political Theory and the Displacement of Politics* (Ithaca, NY: Cornell University Press, 1993), 83.

7
Judith Butler, "Seminar on Hannah Arendt: Eichmann Trials" (European Graduate School, Saas Fee, Switzerland, August 2009).

8
Sven Lütticken, "Fascists Like Us," video statement for *Propositions for Non-Fascist Living*, BAK: Basis voor actuele kunst, 2017, video available here: https://vimeo.com/238275125.

9
Judith Butler, "Can One Lead a Good Life in a Bad Life?," *Radical Philosophy*, no. 176, https://www.radicalphilosophy.com/article/can-one-lead-a-good-life-in-a-bad-life.

10
Nina Power, "Negative Internationalism," 155.

11
Nina Power, "Philosophy, Sexism, Emotion, Rationalism," in *After the Speculative Turn: Realism, Philosophy and Feminism*, ed. Katarina Kolozova & Eileen A. Joy (Brooklyn: Punctum Books, 2016), 18.

12
Donna Haraway, "Situated Knowledges: The Science Question in Feminism and the Privilege of Partial Perspective," in *Feminist Studies* 14, no. 3 (1988): 575–599.

Interview with Wolfgang Tillmans
January 23, 2018, Berlin

In recent years, German artist Wolfgang Tillmans has undertaken projects that engage directly with public politics and discourse, including the ongoing *truth study centre* begun in 2005, and the 2016 poster series aimed against Brexit and toward pro-EU campaigns. *What Is Different?*, the 2018 *Jahresring*—an art yearbook published by the Association of Arts and Culture of the German Economy—was guest-edited by Tillmans and forms the focus of this interview.

Zoë Ritts   I'd like to ask you about *What Is Different?*—how did this project emerge?

Wolfgang Tillmans   It came from a desire to somehow stop just describing the problematic situation we're in, but to analyze and explain why things have changed, and through that understanding enable us with how to deal with the rise of authoritarian politics. Central to the whole phenomenon that we're observing is that authoritarian people and tendencies were kept at bay for the last fifty years, in the West. They were clearly not gone, but somehow from the 1960s onward, authoritarianism was retreating.

Women's rights were progressing and equality was progressing—marginally, but of course in each time it was dramatic. For fifty years progressive sanity, as I would call it, had prevailed, but there is and always have been authoritarian people. At some point I identified them also as assholes. They are diametrically opposed to your idea of equal opportunity.

It's important to see the authoritarian impulse as a personal character trait rather than a left- or right-wing thing, and also tied in with the contrarian character—people who actually are not interested in consensus. I came closer to identifying this is as a mood, a feeling of "Let's smash this consensus." Why didn't they like it in the first place? They had to swallow it in the '70s, '80s, '90s and the noughties. They're always taking offense with things that are rather marginal, like gendered toilets or gender studies, which shows that these questions are emotional.

ZR   Political subjects are psychologically shaped. Essentially the focus of *What Is Different?* is understanding, with the help of psychologists, neuroscientists, and other experts, how these emotional questions shape our identities and political beliefs.

WT   It's not about making better working conditions for millions of people. It's about the sense of loss. There's a beautiful German word *Deutungshoheit*, the power of interpretation or the sovereignty of interpretation. Authoritarian characters feel that there is a permanent crisis, and that everybody else is doing the wrong thing—they are the only ones who have the right answer. They imagine themselves as the rightful leaders of the people, and find it difficult to accept that in Germany's case, they only got 13 percent of the vote. In a secret, free vote, after now a couple of years of intense immigration, propaganda, Trump, and populism, only 13 percent of Germans, in a secret voting booth where they could just suddenly tick AfD, did. Bad enough, but it shows the characteristic [claim] that they keep saying they are bringing their *Volk* back. *What Is Different?* is looking at the actual psychology here. I spoke to people who study the brain, psychologists and neuroscientists, and who try to scientifically understand what actually goes on in truth and lying.

ZR   Could you describe the psychology linked to truth and lying?

WT   The first approach was looking at the "backfire effect." It's a psychological effect that describes that when people who believe in a falsehood are confronted with evidence that contradicts their opinion, they do not actually change their opinion—and it doesn't leave them neutral and unchanged either—but actually strengthens their belief in the falsehood. It seems to be incredibly difficult for the brain to accept or to admit wrongness.

ZR   It's a sort of neurological defense mechanism to resist difficult or conflicting information. A team of scientists you feature argue that "People often discount evidence that contradicts their firmly held beliefs," and used neuroimaging to investigate the neural systems involved in "maintaining belief in the face of counter-evidence" to prove their claims.[1] Could you expand on this?

WT   Yes, admitting that I was wrong seems to be difficult for the brain and the ego, the self; so dangerous that the brain helps the ego by actually finding ways [to turn] truth into a lie, and the other way around. When I heard about that effect and the full extent of it, it became clear to me that this explained conspiracy theorists, who have always been around but are super marginal. If you have suddenly thirty percent of the population not reachable with facts, in certain conditions of voter turnout, those thirty percent can turn into a majority in parliament and can turn into a dictatorship. This effect is not as active as strongly under all circumstances. Facts do and can reach people, but only—and that's the thing—when dispensed by people of your own "side," or whom you somehow trust.

ZR   The digital tribalism that results in the confirmation bias of "only taking in and taking seriously the information that fits into their worldview, while blocking out, discounting, or squarely denying everything else"?

WT   Yes, they found with backfire effect research that it is not always equally effective and opinions can change. But there must be, first and foremost, neural protection for the ego in place. That means certainly for a "Trumpian" that if SkyNews would say climate change is real, then it isn't such a challenge to accept.

ZR   The consensus of findings in *What Is Different?*, between psychologists, scientists, and political actors, is then that the rejection of facts—on an individual level—has become catalyzed as group thinking, when exacerbated by particularly intense current social conditions. Some of your contributors mention a loss of faith in political elites following the 2008 global financial crisis, others point to increasingly difficult social mobility as a result of this and earlier economic factors. Stephan Lewandowsky, the cognitive psychologist with whom you begin the book, speaks of a reduction of social capital and social polarization: "polarization of course is a breeding ground for post-truth. If people are antagonistic and drift further apart, then you're prepared to believe almost anything about your opponent."[2] Which, for you, are the most prominent environmental conditions exacerbating an individual's proclivity to extremism or authoritarianism?

WT   The summary is that when you talk to statisticians, social scientists, and economists etc., everybody will say the world is a better place. More diseases are curable, we don't have the HIV/AIDS crisis anymore in the developed world, we have more safety at work, we have less infant mortality than twenty-five years ago. It isn't true that everything's gotten worse—the facts clearly contradict such pessimistic claims of the populist right.

On the left, too, there is strong belief that everything has become more unjust and more unequal, and of course I am aware that there has been twenty-five years of redistribution from less fortunate to more fortunate people. But when you look at income disparity in Europe, it's not as extreme as it is in America, or China for that matter. There are social, political, economic problems but they are by far not as big.

What has grown strongly is a feeling of uselessness, disconnectedness, and a lack of empowerment, through a media landscape where you're constantly told that you should feel empowered, that you should make a fiction of participation in social media, of influence, instantaneousness, while in reality you're confronted with the same dull life and dull work life that hasn't changed in twenty years.

There are feelings of a lack of a sense of purpose, because society has become more capitalistic and lacking of an alternative social and economic order. In the last twenty-five years things have become more individualistic and all about optimization of the self and the ego. That change left a lack of sense of purpose, in terms of the communal sense. Why the left has not filled that gap, why it has not tried to find answers for those emotions, lies at the heart of the problem. What are we, together?

I saw clubbing and the utopia of nightlife as a powerful political thing in the '90s. That sense of enthusiasm, a sense of purpose, this was new music. New enhanced mental spaces and newly broken-down barriers between European people. We had a sense of "things are gonna get better" after the fall of the Berlin Wall, and it seemed also after the crisis of '80s capitalism, which of course the '90s were not really a pause on. It just was a feeling, and people were not afraid. They were generally looking at a better future. There was a sense of participation. And that's why people were also willing to be tolerant and open to politically correct developments, which I always thought were just that—correct.

ZR   This brings us to the point Carolin Emcke makes about spaces in which to exist safely, about civic spaces dissolving and intimidation increasing in the public sphere. Further, that authoritarian movements in Germany, but also in Poland and Hungary, share a desire to "see the rights of those who live outside of heteronormativity restricted. This hostility has always been there, but not as confidently as it is in public space now." How does this relate to your comments about club culture as communal spaces of difference, successful societal microcosms?

WT   Yes. Actually I did make a small symposium at Tate Modern in the course of my exhibition there last year about the disappearance of public space in terms of youth culture. The centers of most Western cities are no longer nightlife zones. There is no free space, but a lot of surveillance of night life. In the remaining clubs there are security people watching and everything is controlled—capitalism wants that. It wants the idea of attractive, vibrant nightlife. But the reality of a workforce that might be hungover, or that can sign in sick mid-week is just totally unacceptable. Everything has to be healthy.

ZR	This brings us to the notions of purity and disgust, as presented by Philipp Hübl—that the moral principle of "purity" is more valued, and more intrinsic to their political attitudes, for conservatives than for progressives.[3]

WT	Yes. Some took offense to this idea in the project. Here there is a difference between the American term conservative and for example the German *konservativ*, but the idea is that there are certain characteristics that seem to fall in line with certain political preferences.

What [this political, conservative character] needs is a constant air of crisis, and a sense of futurelessness, a fear of future and a future worse than today. Unfortunately, "Capitalism Unhinged" has produced that condition. Capitalist society has atomized people in their feelings and has created an underclass of service deliverers and Deliveroos who maybe were unskilled workers thirty years ago ...

ZR	But perhaps then they were unionized.

WT	Yes, and who now have to live with the lie "I am a self-employed person who chose this." I think you come to an important point which is that this lying to oneself does not come without a price. So many people have to live with illusions "that we have choice," when in fact we don't. In Britain, you're constantly thanked by the train announcements "Thank you for choosing South West Trains," when in fact you don't have a choice other than South West Trains when you live in many parts of the UK. That is a daily pain, a daily price the brain and ego has to pay. We're constantly pushed, being told that we have options, [when in fact] there are no more options. This is deception, and a language of deception that capitalism creates with the air of choices and options that actually are not options.

Many people have no sense of agency about how they can shape their lives. You're treated so disrespectfully by banks, mobile phone companies—that is all capitalism. Every time the brain is told "I'm free," but clearly is not, and suddenly somebody comes in and says your race is better, or your people are better, or your religion is better, and grants an actual sense of empowerment—it's something that you own that cannot be taken away from you, but that others don't have.

ZR Right, an empowerment granted on the basis of fundamental inequality, satiating a desire for social hierarchy—a common element of right-wing extremism being the foundational ideology of inequality.[4]

WT Yes, and that had far less currency fifteen or twenty years ago when there was a sense of all moving toward a better society. That narrative has stopped, ultimately because of globalization, even though it is not completely true.

Globalization is also a good thing, because I feel that fundamentally all humans are born equal, just because you're born in China doesn't mean that you don't have the right to have a car because America says that one billion Chinese can't have a car, that it's just crazy for the climate. We treat everybody equally, and an Indian family can dream of getting a dishwasher or whatnot. Everything we want and take for granted here in Germany we must allow others to want as all.

I think it had to come this way, but this now means there are millions or billions of competitors to otherwise European wide, or American jobs and that is something very threatening.

ZR In keeping with a definition of power as the potential to control possible future realities and looping back to right-wing populism, I'm thinking of what you said about autonomy. There's a frustration, of course, that emerges when alienated from power over one's future—as you're saying, one can see that possibility or a type of freedom to choose exists for others, but are not granted such access. Given these emotional frustrations, people faced with the complex contradictions of life in a globalized, capitalist world react with a threatened response which plays out as xenophobia, racism, scapegoating, and violence.

WT   Exactly that. I think it stems from this frustration that you described, a fiction of the constant self-expression, self-realization diktat. For example, by closing and edging out free communal spaces and introducing more 24/7 work and opening hours, we essentially make people and families less together. We're deprived of a sense of togetherness and soul. Capitalism is not interested in uncontrolled free time without charge or product.

Left wing or center-left wing powers have not described this process of the chipping away at the sense of the communal. The right offers only sport, church, military, and consumption and family values as the providers of communal experiences, whereas solidarity, trade unions, free clubbing, free space were not defended.

Has the art world had any influence? These are big questions, but on the other hand I also certainly don't believe in blowing up the system. Maybe I'm too fearful, but I know that, for example, my life depends upon a functioning pharmaceutical industry and healthcare system. I need certain drugs on a daily basis, and if they blow up everything like some hardcore left-wing people say, well I certainly do not believe in that.

ZR   Long before *What Is Different?* and the posters you made in support of the Brexit "Remain" campaign, your work could be understood as concerned with social investigation, intimate in both private and public. What is your understanding about any social responsibility or role for artists?

WT   I think by definition art is useless. I like to say that provocative sentence because, of course, by useless I mean without purpose, use. Without a declared purpose or use. The very nature of art is that it doesn't have to make sense. It's not pointed research, it's aimless research. That freedom of expression and pointlessness, and the uselessness of art is that it doesn't have to be used, whereas design has a use. I defend artists' right not to get politically involved, having myself become more of an activist, more outspoken directly as a critic. I cannot ask that of my other artist friends more so than of the baker or the car mechanic. But I also realized that no, artists are actually as a whole acting more cowardly in the last twenty years and are neglecting the huge power that art actually has.

Art is hugely powerful. When artists are not afraid to speak to people, they are heard. Most artists are too embarrassed, and they only look at their peer's reactions. Nobody will want to be seen talking at a general understandable level. Everybody hides behind lingo and stays muted and neutered by it in society at large. Many intellectual self-declared left, or self-understanding as left-wing oppositional critical circles are actually totally alien to grassroots activism, to just getting off of their high horse of observer and commentator status.

ZR   And engaging with everyday life.

WT   I understood this aspect of wanting to speak directly through my work and at the same time not dumbing it down. Having complexity and clarity can be a part of the same artist's vocabulary or strategy. I feel a concern for, and interest in, honesty and analysis of rhetoric, and truthfulness and faithfulness of depiction. What happens in presenting our image through clothes, or for example architecture presenting a face of buildings, and hiding the intentions behind their building and cities? The architectural photographs I took [*Book for Architects*, with Rem Koolhaas] are all interested with that sharpening of the eye to detect deception. We must allow or accept that we all play with deception. It's important to detect it in ourselves, including the joys of it. But also then to see the benign forms of deception, and the destructive forms by authoritarian people or authoritarian forms of capital.

ZR   How does the idea of photography as a tool of the construction of multiple social and political realities resonate with you? Especially regarding the direction or redirection of information, something you engaged with in the *truth study centre* by placing real news and fake news side by side.

WT   In the '90s when I first got known there was also a trend of general appreciation of authenticity in photography. And going in parallel also in fashion photography—people who celebrate, say, Nan Goldin as authentic, and Corinne Day's photos of Kate

Moss as somewhat also authentic. I had a completely different take on both, and thought well, of course, nothing is authentic in photography. Authentic is only an absolute term if used in relation to the author's intention. So for example, the picture of Lutz and Alex [*Lutz & Alex sitting in the trees*, 1992] was seen as somehow an authentic picture of my generation. The moment you probe this assumption, just for one split second, it become obvious that of course people didn't sit in trees half-naked. But yet, I don't say this was not an authentic picture, because it is authentic to the intentions of me as the author who wanted to portray a reality in a photograph of an equal, equally empowered gender relationship, and playful use of sexuality. That's what I wanted to embody in these pictures and it seems that I succeeded. That's why they are authentic. But this celebration of photographs that use the language of authenticity as actually authentic, or more authentic than a Helmut Newton picture I totally disbelieve, and want nothing to do with. I've always believed in and have been so fascinated by the construction of the self, of our multifaceted selves. I'm sure that people must have felt that also in decades before, but maybe that is the postmodern experience. That we are more than one.

ZR With social technologies we exist even more simultaneously as these versions of ourselves, our social media selves, our phone-able selves. What did contributors to your volume identify as psychological consequences of that, to our political selves?

WT Now it's that technological hyperreality, but the concept more as a concept existed twenty-five years ago inside me and my friends. You're not just a hippie, but you can also love techno, be a hippie and hate environmental pollution but still be fascinated by the existence of the Concorde airplane. Contradictions were not really allowed, but they were still there. The reconciliation of the coexistence of contradictory parts of oneself are problematic. How one is constantly part of the problem and entangled in it. That seemed to me the principle experience of the current of my time and self, especially with the claims and counterclaims on photography and authenticity.

ZR   This brings us to the conclusion of one reaction against complexity as, for some, a move to political subjecthood based on reduced or simplified information or truths. Authoritarianism as a psychologically helpful response to complex identities in a complex world.

WT   Yes, and that's how we have to close—with this statement. I'm glad that you bring it back to that. In the *What Is Different?* interviews, I asked occasionally how we could make complexity more attractive. My work is a celebration of that complexity, in its greatest clarity, and uses affirmation rather than complication, criticism and finger-pointing. I think complexity will always win. So far every dictatorship has fallen, every theocracy has fallen. Complexity and the reality of people being different will win.

ZR   So we can be optimistic!

WT   Yes! We have to. Because I tell you, it wasn't so great back then. And now talking occasionally to twenty-five year olds who have this rose-tinted idea of '90s, and of course it wasn't all better. It was just the sense of purpose, I think, that is lacking now. And that doesn't have to be absent, because there is a lot of purpose now to rally and come together!
      In addition to what has changed, and what is the effectively causing these reactions, there's something I observed which I describe as the violence of advertising. It is so inescapable and so unchallenged. For example the Tag Heuer brand says, in their advertising, something like "Don't get to the breaking point." In London it's everywhere, and people are actually at breaking point—and constantly seeing "don't." With this luxury product you don't get to breaking point. It is a violence to be constantly shown inequality or unattainability of what is being spelled out as essential to have, and this creates unhappiness. Maybe one day those who designed all these messages, and those who paid and ordered these messages will have to answer for how much unhappiness they created in people with these pictures of desire and the proliferation of desire.

1
Jonas T. Kaplan, Sarah I. Gimbel, and Sam Harris, "Neural Correlates of Maintaining One's Political Beliefs in the Face of Counterevidence," in *What Is Different?: Jahresring* 64, ed. Wolfgang Tillmans (Berlin: Sternberg Press, 2018), 78.

2
Wolfgang Tillmans, "Interview with Stephan Lewandowsky," in *What Is Different?*, 14.

3
Philipp Hübl, "The Power of Political Emotions: On Political Camp Formation and the New Right-Wing Populism," in *What Is Different?*, 36.

4
Wolfgang Tillmans, "Interview with Bianca Klose," in *What Is Different?*, 59.

Let's Talk about Fascism
Hito Steyerl

Yes, I mean it. Not about psychology or evil as such. Not about insanity or sudden unpredictable doom. You are trying to avoid the topic. The topic is fascism.

We have seen a similar avoidance after the attacks in Oslo and on Utøya. As if societies did not want to trust their own eyes and ears. The perpetrator has extensively articulated his neo-fascist beliefs. Yet people are trying to avoid this fact. His act is not called an act of terror, but of lunacy. It is depoliticized and represented as a private deviation that unexpectedly struck the country like a natural disaster. It is thus divorced from the political dimension and becomes a private, individual action.

But this avoidance has something more to tell us. It points to a gap in representation itself. It originates in very serious epistemological and political issues that are worked deep into the fabric of contemporary fascism and its resurgence across Europe and beyond. More than this: they are embedded very fundamentally in the ways in which we perceive contemporary reality.

The fundamental problem is not a lack of morals, though. Nor is it a question of good or evil, sanity or illness. It is the issue of representation. On the one hand political representation, on the other cultural representation; and in fact, thirdly, of economic participation. What do all of these have to do with the public reactions to the massacre?

Political Representation

So what are political representation and cultural representation? More precisely: What are the disparities between and within these concepts? They rest on contradictions that are irresolvable; and fascism seems to be a convenient jump cut to an attempt to explode these different aporias. Let's start with the basics. Political representation in a liberal democracy is gained mainly by participation in the electoral process. This requires citizenship. True political representation is thus inadequate in all European democracies.

This is well known. But there are much more general and pressing issues now. Political power is increasingly being eroded. Who achieves or doesn't achieve political representation matters less and less. Even people with full political privileges, members of parties—even parliaments—are increasingly ignored. Because whatever the people want, whoever they are, and regardless of who represents them, the contemporary sovereigns are mainly the "markets." The markets, not the people, are to be appeased, satisfied, and pleased by the political class. In the area of economics, representation exists too. Participation in economic processes is measured by the abilities to get credit, to own, and to consume. This also explains the contemporary rage against what is essentially economic or consumer exclusion. Many contemporary riots do not have political goals—why should they, since political action proves powerless in many cases?—but strive for economic participation: the most concentrated expression of this is the looting of shopping malls.

This erosion of political power is a result of decades of redistribution of wealth, opportunity, and actual power from the poor to the rich. While it was possible, the poor were appeased with credit and indentured shopping. Now that this no longer seems to work, economic participation has become a battleground.

But what does all this have to do with fascism? On the surface, nothing. But these phenomena are all symptoms of what could tentatively be called post-democracy. In post-democracy, politics is successively abandoned as a means of organizing the common.

Post-democracy is also felt within political institutions. Citizens of the European Union, for example, are faced with a host of institutions that are not democratically legitimized (among these, again, financial institutions, which are not subject to any political control). The votes of citizens do not have the same weight, depending on their citizenship, thus creating different classes of political representation. Within Europe and beyond, oligarchies of all kinds are on the rise. Retreating bureaucracies are replaced with authoritarian rule, tribal rackets, and organized vigilantism. The so-called monopoly of violence is increasingly privatized, handed over to private armies, security companies, and outsourced gangs. Forces that could be controlled democratically are weakening, while states and other actors impose their agendas through emergency powers or "necessity." There have been so many examples of this over the last few decades that I don't even want to start listing them.

All of these symptoms intensify anxieties around the idea of political representation as such. Weren't we promised equality? Yes, we were. Wasn't the idea of democracy that we'd all be represented? No, we aren't. Political representation involves a certain arbitrariness and randomness—to a certain extent they are inherent in it, but they seem to be accelerating at a tremendous rate right now. It involves instability, unpredictability, and a large dose of futility.

Cultural Representation

So how about cultural representation, then? What is it anyway? Cultural representation is (in many cases, visual) representation in the public realm. Via texts, advertisements, popular culture, TV—you name it. We don't need to go into this, you only have to look around you. The situation appears to be quite different here. There is an overabundance of representation of almost anything and anybody: in commercial as well as social media. This avalanche of representation has increased a great deal with digital technologies. That things and people are represented culturally doesn't mean much, though. It just means that lots of images are floating around, hustling for attention.

What is the relation, then, between political and cultural representation? Between *Darstellung* und *Vertretung*, or between proxy and portrait, as Gayatri Spivak put it?

There is one. But it isn't the one that has traditionally been assumed to exist. Some thirty to forty years ago, early Cultural

Studies, with its Gramscian implications, understood cultural representation as some sort of visual democracy. The assumption went something like this: if people were represented culturally in a positive way, political equality would become more likely. Passionate battles over the idea of a politics of representation characterized a large part of the '80s (and in many places, way beyond them).

But we are now realizing that something in this equation went wrong; or, to put it more neutrally, something changed dramatically. While cultural representation of everything is undergoing massive inflation (coupled with the devaluation and degradation of most individual images, texts, and sounds) political representation is not only uneven, it is also less and less relevant. The two realms also seem to be running wildly out of sync. The period of the exponential growth of all things represented, the era of the proliferation of circulating images and data, is also the period of the radicalization of anti-immigration policies, the institution of increasingly harsh border regimes, the growth of neo-fascist (some prefer to call them right-wing populist) movements and parties, and a general loss of the authority of politics.

If one were to push the point, one could conclude that there is almost an inversely proportional relationship between political and cultural representation. The more people are represented culturally, and the more they snap one another on their cellphones and submit to Facebook surveillance schemes, the less they matter politically. But this may be only partly the case. The real link is perhaps that both types function perfectly erratically and unevenly. They are both more portraits than proxies, and not necessarily very good portraits either.

The Collapse of Representation

And now the refusal to acknowledge fascism, even though it is proclaimed publicly and backed up with atrocities, as in the case of the attacks in Oslo and Utøya, becomes clearer—because this avoidance points to a blind spot that links the problem of representation with fascism.

Why is this so? It is because in fascism, representation collapses. It is short-circuited by attempts to avoid all the complications inherent in it, and to label representation as an alien and foreign concept. Fascism claims to express the essence of the people by imposing a leader and by replacing cultural representation with caricatures passed off as simple truth. It tries to get rid of representation altogether.

And indeed there are many reasons to be suspicious of contemporary representation. In both political and cultural representation, the link between represented and representation seems to have become dramatically more complicated in recent years, and it very often disintegrates completely. Representation, as we know it, is heading for a crash—or rather it is nose-diving in a vertiginous tailspin.

In cultural representation, the concept of reality has been stressed to an unprecedented extent. Many of the rules and conventions of visual representation have become almost obsolete with the recent digital revolution. In the case of pictures, the so-called indexical bond of photography (which was always dubious) has been shattered by copy-and-paste technologies, accelerated fog-of-war campaigns, and unprecedented opportunities for scams, misinformation, and deceit. Traditional truth-testing procedures—journalistic, legal, and to some extent also scientific— have been replaced by digital rumor, widespread deregulation, the law of demand, and Wikipedia-like, crowdsourced "knowledge." Of course, cultural representation has always been tricky. But the emergence of fascism 2.0 speaks to a period in which digital rancor can spread like wildfire, fueled by avatars who can hardly be linked to real people anymore. Just as representation as such has been untethered from institutional control, its content has in many cases been divorced from any empirical reality. Don't get me wrong. I don't think the digital revolution is a bad thing. On the contrary, it has enabled many great advances in the free circulation of information. But at the cost of increased uncertainty and instability. There is no denying this either.

In political representation, one of the major realizations of recent years is that even those who are politically represented feel powerless, as power today seems to be coded more economically than politically. So, ironically, political representation starts to resemble cultural representation. It becomes more portrait than proxy, while its internal contradictions increase. Complications thus intensify, with both political and cultural representation.

Finance and Epistemology

Maybe the common denominator of all these diverse slippages in representation is the notion of speculation. Speculation is at once a financial and an epistemological tool. In finance, speculation means to take a step whose implications cannot be safely predicted. Not all the information is (or can be) available at the time of taking the decision. Risk is thus increased, but presumably so is opportunity. Speculation also means that value is increasingly unhitched from the object to which it refers. It does not refer to the thing in question any more, but to the context of its circulation and the affects attached to it. It represents mood swings around derivatives of derivatives. It is more like video feedback from a wildly agitated hand-held camera feed than a conventional still-image illustration (and by this I do not mean to imply that the latter is more truthful than the former—just more predictable).

It is not difficult to see how this relates to speculation as a tool of observation and research. *Speculari* means to observe in Latin. It is used as the Latin translation of the Greek *theoria* and describes the quest for the essence or origins of things behind their empirical existence. At the same time, it refers to a jump into the haze of pure appearance, as Augustine's reflections on the recognition of God in a dark mirror suggest. According to Hans Reichenbach, speculation characterizes periods of transition in philosophy, when the questions exceed the possible rational means of answering them. Thus philosophical speculation also presents risks and opportunities. It presents the possibility of thinking outside the box as well as the danger of getting completely lost out there.

But speculation has also come to characterize many vernacular processes of representation. All the things that are not known, but are suspected. All the rumors that are not substantiated. All the complexity compressed beyond recognition. Viral videos, whose circulation multiplies in bubbles of representation, with a thick coating of affect dripping from them. Grainy, abstract footage from war zones. The addiction to emergency and catastrophe, and their subsequent inflation on exponentially multiplying screens. The loss of confidence in images and any other referential values and their relation to whatever they refer to.

Many of the processes that characterize speculation in general—above all its risky and unsubstantiated relation to reality—are inherent in digital representation practices. Representation as such is extremely dynamized by speculation. The result is that the relation between referent and sign, between person and proxy, becomes extremely unpredictable—like many other contemporary phenomena. Speculation turbocharges representation; it accelerates the tailspin that we are living through today.

This is not solely bad news. Speculation as a method opens up new freedoms of expression and thought, which, on the other hand, can easily be put to terrible use. Opportunities arise by the minute—and realities are wasted and destroyed at the same time. This opens up new horizons of thinking, which in many cases end up as complete delusions. Speculation is a harbinger of possibility and exploration, just as it plays into bigotry and bias.

This is where fascism comes into play. Where representation collapses or spins off into precipitous loops and feedbacks, fascism seemingly offers easy answers. It is the panic button for blocking off annoying remnants of reality.

By apparently doing away with the complications of representation, fascism manages to obfuscate that it is the highest form of contemporary speculative representation: its point of collapse, or of impact. The crash itself is at once overrepresented and unrepresented. A blind spot filled with delusion and death. The irreversible parting of the ways with empirical reality.

The good news for fascists is that their ideology is so compatible with contemporary economic paradigms—because it resonates perfectly with an ideology in which society is nothing and the individual's greed and will to power are everything. In which tribe and racket rule supreme and flattened stereotypes hyperventilate. Especially in an era of first-person shooter games and online fanaticism, fascism seems like an ideal complement to "overdrive capitalism": a built-in competitive advantage for Aryans. Not only does it promise to reintroduce a (completely speculative) referent for value, namely race or culture, conveniently, it also promises its target audience that they will be in the upper echelon of the class divide, because dirty and low-paid jobs will be dumped on "subhumans." It presents a seeming alternative to the brutal equality of liberal democracy in which everybody is presumed to "make it" or fail, by presenting itself as self-evident "truth." In fascism, the abstract equality of capitalist liberalism is abolished by the collapse of class into race. It is a perfect ideology for lazy Aryans: you enjoy all the benefits of capitalism without actually having to work.

At this point we recognize that the words "Aryan" and "race" can be replaced with other copy-and-paste jargons that share similar premises. Most terror attacks of the last decade have actually been initiated by right-wing extremists who want their respective cultures to remain "pure" and exclusive, who hate women, communists, and most minorities (minorities from their point of view, that is) and cook up an ideology centered around testosterone-driven masculinity. Not all of these ideologies are fascist, and there is no point trying to boil them all down to this notion. But all of them try to replace equality by uniformity—however they define the latter.

But here is the point. None of what I have written about necessarily leads to fascism. It presents the context that facilitates its emergence: it doesn't inevitably lead to it. The reason is simple. People have the choice. Anybody can choose to become a fascist or not. And most people, thankfully, have so far chosen not to.

And one can also choose not to ignore the problem. Instead of denying these challenges, we should face up to them. We should face up to the complete unhinging of reality by reintroducing checks and balances, by renegotiating value and information, by insisting on representation and human solidarity. This also includes acknowledging and opposing real existing fascism and its countless derivatives and franchises. Denying its existence means surrendering to a newly emerging paradigm of post-politics and post-democracy; to a complete turning-away from reality.

This essay is a reprint of Hito Steyerl, "Let's Talk about Fascism," in *Duty Free Art: Art in the Age of Planetary Civil War* (London: Verso, 2017), 171–180.

The Stone

Markus Miessen & Zoë Ritts

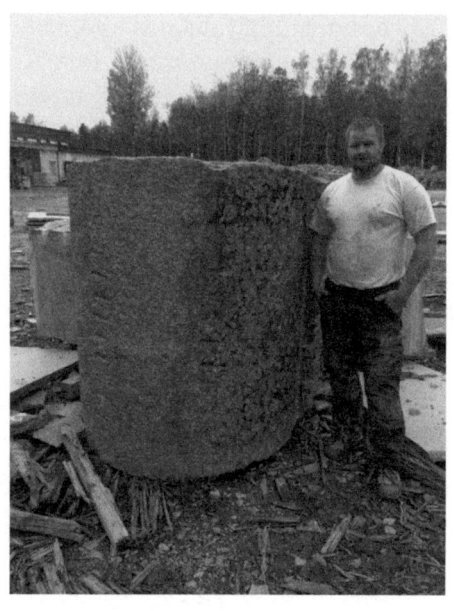

We heard about it by chance. A quarry in Sweden had mined granite during the Third Reich for one of architect Wilhelm Kreis's later projects, the unbuilt *Soldatenhalle*, part of the *Oberkommando des Heeres*. Post-war overstock had been moved and redistributed among other quarries in Sweden, including one currently in operation that we might be able to reach.

Third Reich architects had originally commissioned stone mined from forced labor quarries in Norway during the war. Moving operations to Sweden, the Nazis ordered native red Bohus granite cut for massive cornices and decorative columns to use for projects like the *Soldatenhalle*. As per procedure, all the granite pieces cut parts were marked, dated, and approved by a Third Reich officer. Some pieces were rejected due to minor defects, left for other uses and eventually inherited by our contact in Sweden.

As Björn Nordenhake, the quarry manager, explained, he had received four pieces rejected by the wartime government, due to minor errors in their drill-markings. These blocks, including a sculpted rectangular volume over 200 cm in length and part of a column measuring 150 cm in height and 120 cm in diameter, were rough-formed with pins and wedges, fine-formed by hand with a point chisel. The stone is black, white, and red in color, unassuming save for the occasional glint of reflection—and its heavy history.

The stone perfectly exemplified for us the translation of politics into architecture. In doing so, it represented the foundational conceit of the entire "Design Politics" project from which this book departs: that material itself is not neutral, that design is weighted with the political. A single rectangle of granite crystallized, through its provenance, production, and even geological origin, the haptic material of a world-changing historical and political moment. The Third Reich, like movements before and since, conveyed their politics through printed symbol and monolithic, representational architecture, design at and beyond the scale of the body and of the city.

Actually getting the stone from the quarry in Sweden would not be as clear-cut. Our first intention was to use several sections of the granite as the bar top for the *Para-Politics* symposium that we were organizing in Gothenburg, Sweden, as part of the Design Festival in November 2017. Practical considerations of time and shipping limited that possibility, and eventually we modified our design to use a single smaller piece of granite as the entry threshold piece of the bar and symposium space. Instead of resting drinks on the granite bar top, the stone would act as a threshold. But as the symposium approached, there was no sign of the stone that the quarry manager had kindly shipped. When we finally reached the Swedish shipping company Post-Nord, we discovered that the package was sitting in a truck somewhere between Sibbhult and Gothenburg, and wouldn't arrive in time—so we held the symposium without it. In the weeks that followed, the stone's location was still a mystery, and increasingly this piece of granite became a bit of a myth. Supposedly, it had arrived in the city; supposedly, it had been moved to a holding facility; but after increasingly comical phone calls and attempts to find it, the stone was retrieved by a colleague at HDK. Almost two months after Björn shipped it to us for the symposium, we opened the package in the HDK mailroom to finally see the fabled stone—only to find it broken in three pieces.

This strange saga inspired a series of studio photographs by Enric Duch, and later a new work by Liam Gillick commissioned for this book.

Even for a studio based in Berlin, a city of stone where the physical traces of a long material history are everywhere—nevertheless often hidden, erased, or reconstructed—the significance of this object is an important reminder that politics are a spatial concern, and indeed, spatial design is always political. To that end, any contemporary designer is no less implicated in a larger question of this relationship than even an extreme historical example shows. This book brings together voices cognizant of that reality, working to understand the ways in which our current political landscape is built of such structures and materials—and how, given that, we as designers might work.

To Fit Reality to Their Lies, 2018
Liam Gillick

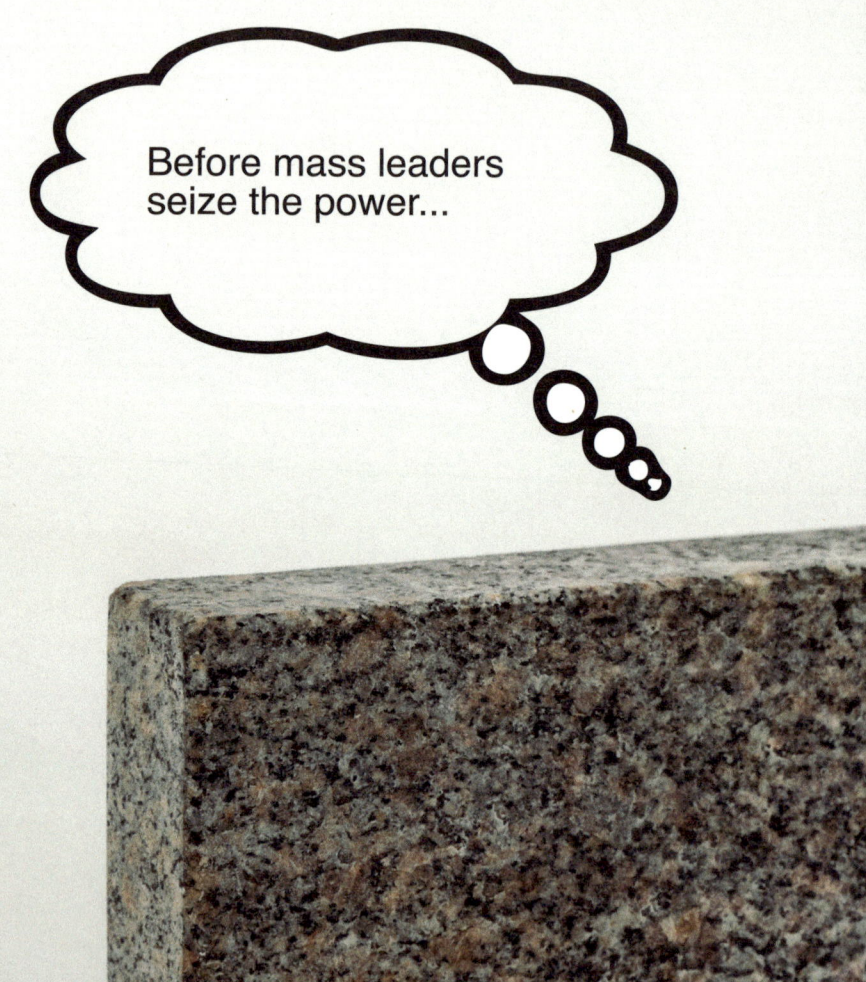

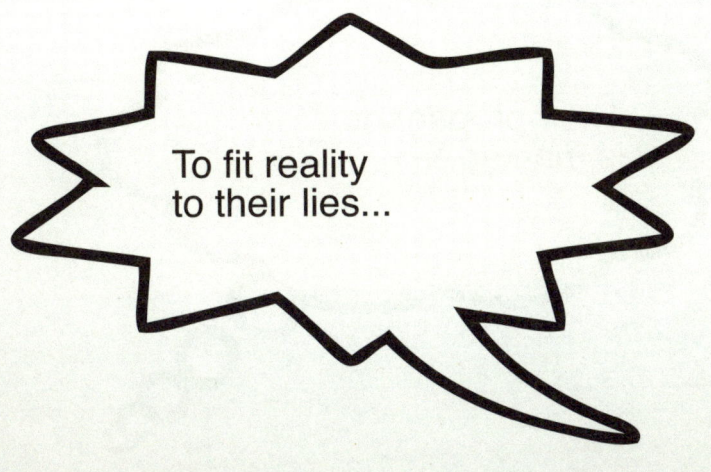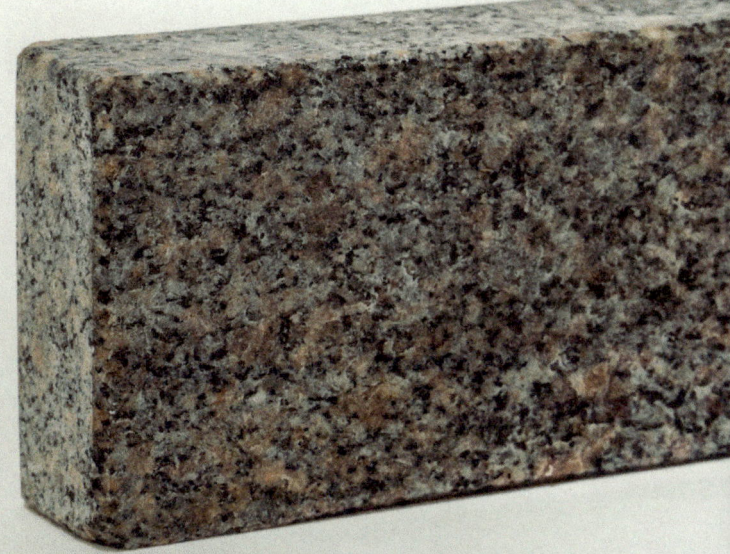

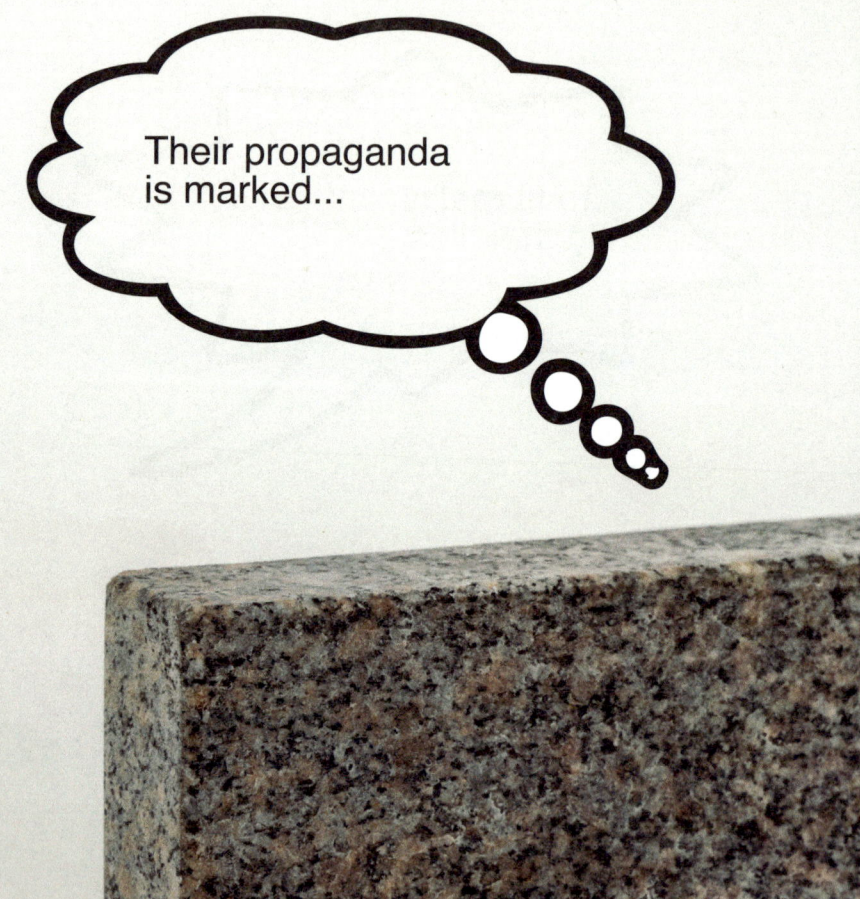

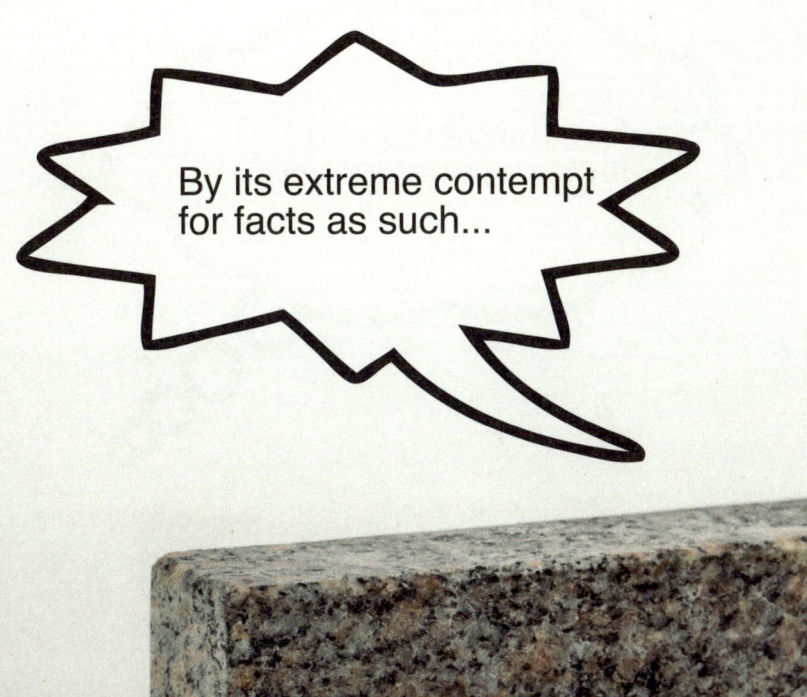

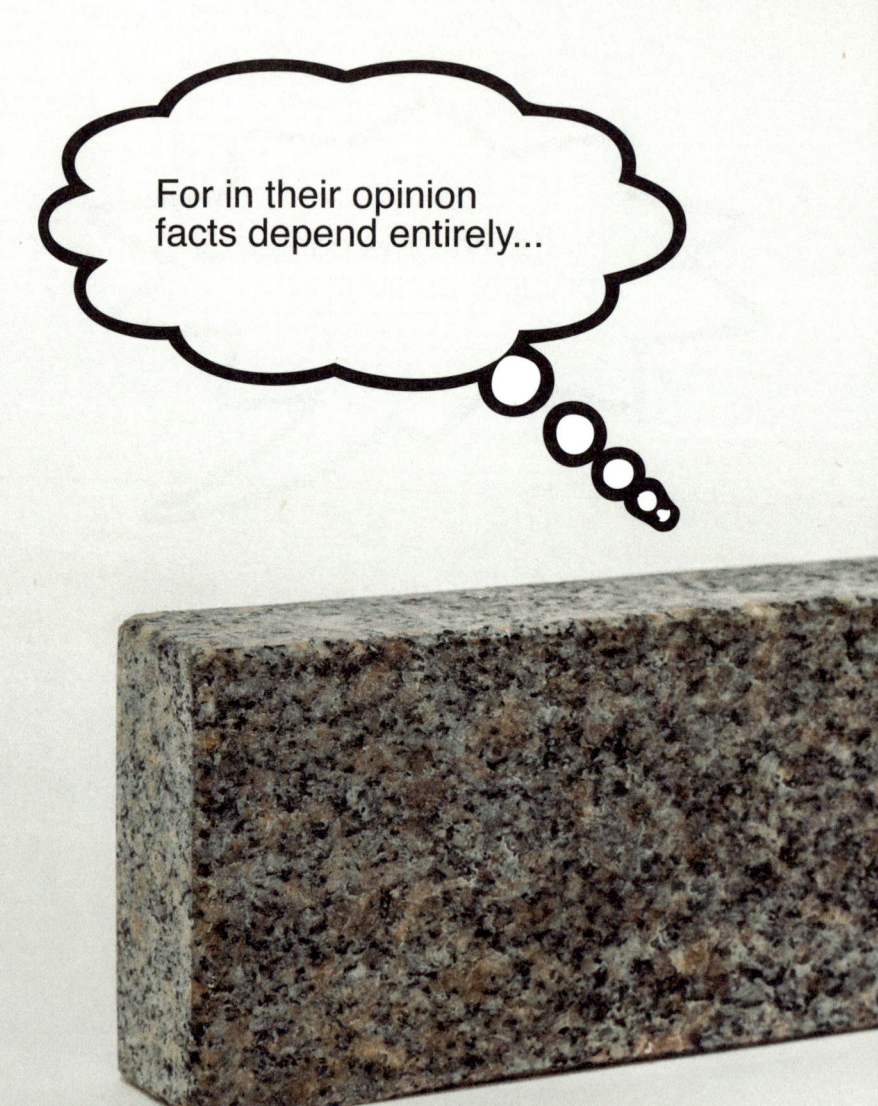

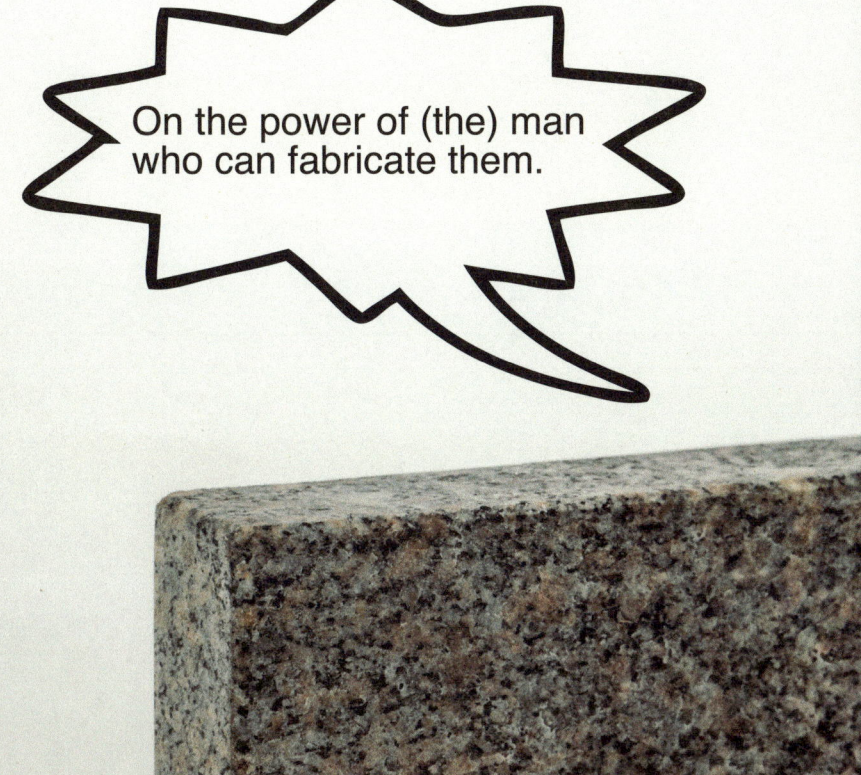

Biographies

Benjamin H. Bratton's work spans philosophy, art, design, and computer science. He is Professor of Visual Arts and Director of the Center for Design and Geopolitics at the University of California, San Diego. He is Program Director of the Strelka Institute of Media, Architecture and Design in Moscow, and Visiting Faculty at SCI-Arc, Los Angeles. In *The Stack: On Software and Sovereignty* (2016) Bratton outlines a new theory for the age of global computation and algorithmic governance. *Dispute Plan to Prevent Future Luxury Constitution* (2015) weaves fact and fiction to dramatize the symmetries and complicities between designed violence and the violence of design. His current research project, Theory and Design in the Age of Machine Intelligence, is on the unexpected and uncomfortable design challenges posed by AI in various guises: from machine vision to synthetic cognition and sensation, and the macroeconomics of robotics to everyday geoengineering.

Liam Gillick deploys multiple forms to expose the new ideological control systems that emerged at the beginning of the 1990s. Gillick's work exposes the dysfunctional aspects of a modernist legacy in terms of abstraction and architecture when framed within a globalized, neoliberal consensus. His work extends into structural rethinking of the exhibition as a form. He has produced a number of short films since the late 2000s, *Margin Time* (2012), *The Heavenly Lagoon* (2013), and *Hamilton: A Film by Liam Gillick* (2014). The book *Industry and Intelligence: Contemporary Art since 1820* was published by Columbia University Press in 2016. Gillick's work has been included in numerous important exhibitions including documenta and the Venice, Berlin, and Istanbul Biennales—representing Germany in 2009 in Venice. Solo museum exhibitions have taken place at the Museum of Contemporary Art in Chicago, the Museum of Modern Art in New York, and Tate in London.

Hannes Grassegger is an economist and reporter based in Zurich, Switzerland. His writing centers around how digitalization transforms the way we live. He is known for his investigations on Cyberwarfare, Cambridge Analytica, and the Facebook censorship system. In 2014 he published his first book *Das Kapital bin Ich* (I am Capital), arguing that we should become the sole owners of our data. Hannes works as a reporter for *Das Magazin* (Zurich). He has won several awards for journalism and is a fellow at the Wilson Center in Washington, DC. His work has been translated into over twenty languages and published via *Pro Publica, Guardian, New Republic, Süddeutsche Zeitung Magazin, NZZ, Internazionale, VICE, Die ZEIT, Revue XXI* etc. In 2018, Grassegger received the Wächterpreis der deutschen Tagespresse.

Mahmoud Keshavarz is a postdoctoral researcher at the Engaging Vulnerability Research Program, Department of Cultural Anthropology and Ethnology, Uppsala University. He has been a Visiting Scholar at Parsons School of Design and the University of Gothenburg. His research and publications sit at the intersection of design studies and politics of movement and migration. His book *The Design Politics of the Passport: Materiality, Immobility and Dissent* was published in 2018 with Bloomsbury Academic. He is cofounder and member of the Decolonising Design Group.

Markus Miessen is a Berlin-based architect, writer, and professor at the Academy of Design, University of Gothenburg, Sweden. He received his PhD from the Centre for Research Architecture at Goldsmiths, London. The initiator of the Participation tetralogy, his work revolves around questions of critical spatial practice, institution building, and spatial politics. Miessen has previously taught at the Architectural Association, London, and has been a Harvard Fellow. Most recently, he has held a Stiftungsprofessur for Critical Spatial Practice at the Städelschule, Frankfurt, and was Distinguished Professor of Practice at USC, Los Angeles. Among many other books and writings, Miessen is the author of *The Nightmare of Participation* (2011) and *Crossbenching* (2016). His architectural design practice, Studio Miessen, works closely with a number of artists such as Hito Steyerl and Flaka Haliti, and is currently involved in the spatial re-conceptualization of the Martin Gropius Bau, Berlin, under the new directorship of Stephanie Rosenthal.

Angela Nagle is the author of the best seller *Kill All Normies: Online Culture Wars from 4chan and Tumblr to Trump and the Alt-Right*. She writes for *The Atlantic*, *Jacobin*, and *The Baffler*. Her PhD research was on online antifeminist politics and subcultures, and she was also coeditor of *Ireland under Austerity* with Manchester University Press. *Kill All Normies* was voted among the *Guardian*'s books of the year in 2017 by novelist George Saunders and she has been praised as "one of the brightest lights in a new generation of left writers and thinkers who have declared their independence from intellectual conformity."

Nina Power is a cultural critic, social theorist, and a Senior Lecturer in Philosophy at the University of Roehampton, London. She received her PhD in Philosophy from Middlesex University. She is the author of *One Dimensional Woman* and has written widely on feminism, activism, art, culture, labor and care. Power also served as both editor and translator of Alain Badiou's *On Beckett*. Her work has been published in magazines and newspapers like *Radical Philosophy*, *Wire*, *frieze*, and *Guardian*. Power is also a Tutor in Critical Writing in Art and Design at the Royal College of Art, London. In 2015, she commissioned *Bad Feelings* by Arts Against Cuts, a collection of writing and "set of materials for conflict and commonality" published by Book Works.

Patricia Reed is an artist, writer, and designer based in Berlin. As an artist, selected exhibitions include those at the Museum of Capitalism, Oakland; Homeworks 7, Beirut; Witte de With, Rotterdam; HKW, Berlin; and Württembergischer Kunstverein, Stuttgart. Recent writings have been published in *e-flux Architecture*; *Xeno-Architecture*; *_AH Journal*; *Cold War Cold World*; *Reinventing Horizons*; *Moneylab 2*; and *The Neurotic Turn*. With Victoria Ivanova, she cocurated the *1948 Unbound: Tokens* session as a performative symposium with the Haus der Kulturen der Welt team, Berlin (2017), and is currently a theory researcher for Public Art Munich 2018. Reed is also part of the Laboria Cuboniks (techno-material feminist) working group.

Konrad Renner has been Professor of Digitale Grafik at the Hochschule für bildende Kunst Hamburg since 2017, together with Christoph Knoth. Previously, he taught Interface Design at the Berlin University of the Arts, and worked for three years before that for the Master's Programme Editorial Design of the Burg Giebichenstein University of Art and Design Halle, and for two semesters, together with Christoph Knoth, at Bauhaus-Universität Weimar, where they launched the project Digital Typography. After working for Projects Projects in New York, they founded the studio Knoth & Renner in Berlin and Leipzig in 2011. Since then, they have developed projects for the architectural journal *Arch+*; publishers Spector Books, the Academy of Fine Arts Leipzig, Werkleitz Halle and Casco Utrecht; the pavilions of New Zealand and Germany at the Venice Biennale in 2015; and Arbeitsgemeinschaft Deutscher Kunstvereine.

Zoë Ritts is an architectural designer based in Berlin. She holds an M. Arch (2017) from the Rhode Island School of Design, where she received the American Institute of Architects Henry Fernandez Award for History and Theory. She is also a graduate of Concordia University, with a BA/BFA (2013) in History and Fine Arts. She has worked in varied architectural, cultural, and curatorial settings.

Slavs & Tatars is an internationally-renowned art collective devoted to an area east of the former Berlin Wall and west of the Great Wall of China known as Eurasia. Their work has been the subject of solo exhibitions at the Museum of Modern Art, NY; Salt, Istanbul; Vienna Secession, Kunsthalle Zürich, and Ujazdowski Centre for Contemporary Art, Warsaw. The collective's practice is based on three activities: exhibitions, publications, and lecture-performances. Slavs & Tatars have published eight books to date, including *Mirrors for Princes* (2015), *Not Moscow Not Mecca* (2012), as well as their translation of the legendary Azerbaijani satirical periodical *Molla Nasreddin*.

Jonas Staal is an artist and founder of the artistic and political organization New World Summit and the campaign New Unions. Staal's work includes interventions in public space, exhibitions, theater plays, publications, and lectures, focusing on the relationship between art, democracy, and propaganda. Recent solo exhibitions include "Art of the Stateless State" (Moderna Galerija, Ljubljana, 2015), "After Europe" (State of Concept, Athens, 2016), "Museum as Parliament" (Van Abbemuseum, Eindhoven, 2018, in collaboration with the Democratic Federation of North-Syria) and "Steve Bannon: A Propaganda Retrospective" (Het Nieuwe Instituut, Rotterdam, 2018). His projects have been exhibited widely, among others at the 7th Berlin Biennial (2012), the 31st São Paulo Biennale (2014), the Oslo Architecture Triennial (2016), and the Gothenburg Biennial (2017). Books by Staal include *Nosso Lar, Brasília* (Jap Sam Books, 2014), and *Stateless Democracy* (BAK, basis voor actuele kunst, Utrecht, 2015). He completed his PhD on *Propaganda Art from the 20th to the 21st Century* at the PhDArts program of the University of Leiden.

Hito Steyerl is Professor of Experimental Film and Video and the cofounder of the Research Center for Proxy Politics at the Berlin University of the Arts. She studied cinematography and documentary film in Tokyo and Munich and wrote her doctoral thesis at the Academy of Fine Arts in Vienna. Her research focuses on media, technology, and the distribution of images. In her texts, performances, and documentary-essay films Hito Steyerl deals with the postcolonial and feminist criticism of representational logic. She works at the intersections of visual art and film as well as theory and practice. Her numerous works have been exhibited at the most prominent global art institutions, such as the Venice Biennale, the Museum of Contemporary Art, Los Angeles, and the Museum of Modern Art, New York. In addition to her work as an artist she was a lecturer at the Center for Cultural Studies at Goldsmiths College in London and a guest professor at the Royal Academy of Copenhagen and the Academy of Fine Arts, Helsinki. The Royal College of Art, London, honored her in 2016 with an "Honorary Doctorate."

Wolfgang Tillmans lives and works in Berlin and London. In 2000, he was the first photographer and first non-British artist to win the Turner Prize. In 2015, he received the Hasselblad Foundation International Award in Photography, and in January 2018, he was awarded the Kaiserring prize from the city of Goslar in Germany. His work has been the subject of many international solo exhibitions. Tillmans's work has also been included in significant survey exhibitions including Manifesta 10, the State Hermitage Museum, St. Petersburg (2014), "Fundamentals, the 14th International Architecture Biennal" directed by Rem Koolhaas, Venice Biennale (2014), Berlin Biennale (1998, 2014), the 3rd Moscow Biennale of Contemporary Art, Russia (2009), and the 51st and 53rd Venice Biennales (2005, 2009). In recent years, Tillmans has been more directly involved in political activism. In tandem with his ongoing *truth study centre* (begun in 2005), he has created posters for an anti-Brexit / pro-EU campaign in 2016 and in response to rightwing populism in Germany in advance of the federal elections in 2017.

Stephan Trüby is professor for architecture and cultural theory, and director of the institute Grundlagen moderner Architektur und Entwerfen (IGMA) at the University of Stuttgart. He studied architecture at the Architectural Association in London and has taught at Hochschule für Gestaltung (HfG) in Karlsruhe, Zürcher Hochschule der Künste (ZHdK), Graduate School of Design (GSD) at Harvard University, and at TU München. Among his most important publications are *Exit-Architektur: Design zwischen Krieg und Frieden* (2008), *The World of Madelon Vriesendorp* (2008, with Shumon Basar), *Die deutschen Beitrage zur Architekturbiennale Venedig seit 1991 – Eine Oral History* (2016, with Verena Hartbaum), *Absolute Architekturbeginner: Schriften 2004–2014* (2017), and *Die Geschichte des Korridors* (2018). He is currently working on a book about rightwing spaces in Europe, Russia, and the United States.

Christina Varvia is an architect researcher and the Deputy Director of Forensic Architecture. She graduated from the AA School of Architecture with a previous degree from Westminster University. Her previous research includes studies on digital media and memory as well as the perception of the physical environment through scanning and imaging technologies, research that she deploys through time-based media. Varvia has worked in architectural practice and was part of the Unknown Fields Division before she joined the Forensic Architecture (FA) team in 2014. In FA she has developed methodologies and coordinated the *Rafah: Black Friday* report, unpacking one day of war in Gaza, 2014, *Saydnaya: Inside a Syrian Torture Prison Project, 77sqm_9:26min: A Counter Investigation*, as well as many other projects and exhibitions.

Image Credits

pp. 41, 47: Courtesy of Benjamin H. Bratton

pp. 54–55: Courtesy of Slavs & Tatars

pp. 58–132: Symposium

>Fig. 1
Fredrik Sandberg / TT via AP Hannes, Symposium

>Fig. 2
Courtesy of Gui Bonsiepe

>Fig. 3
Courtesy of Wikimedia Commons

>Figs. 4, 5
Courtesy of Hannes Grassegger

>Fig. 6
Courtesy of Luma Partners

>Figs. 7–15
Courtesy of Stephan Trüby

>Figs. 16–21
Courtesy of Forensic Architecture

pp. 136–137: Courtesy of Konrad Renner

p. 149: Courtesy of Remco van Bladel and Jonas Staal

pp. 150–151: Courtesy of Jonas Staal

p. 186: Courtesy of Björn Nordenhake

pp. 190–195: Artwork courtesy of Liam Gillick / Original photography by Enric Duch

Acknowledgments

The editors would like to thank HDK Academy of Design in Gothenburg for their enthusiasm and support of the project and events. Moreover, we are indebted to HDK faculty, Studio NOCK, and everyone else who helped facilitate the November 2017 symposium at SPÄTI BAR as part of the Gothenburg Design Festival / Open Week: Onkar Kular as curator in chief, Matthias Gunnarsson, Johnny Friberg, and our speakers that day: Christina Varvia, Hannes Grassegger, and Stephan Trüby.

We are grateful for the enthusiasm of our generous contributors: Benjamin H. Bratton, Liam Gillick, Hannes Grassegger, Mahmoud Keshavarz, Kasia Korczak, Angela Nagle, Nina Power, Patricia Reed, Konrad Renner, Payam Sharifi, Jonas Staal, Hito Steyerl, Wolfgang Tillmans and Shahin Zarinbal, Stephan Trüby, and Christina Varvia.

We are also indebted to Arno Brandlhuber and studio Brandlhuber+ for the poster project which informed and inspired the cover and color palette of this volume. See opposite page.

We would like to thank Florian Slotawa for putting us in touch with Claes Nordenhake. Thanks to Björn Nordenhake for sharing your knowledge with us and—finally—for sending us a very important piece of stone.

There are countless individuals and sparring partners with whom we have had and continue to have important and productive exchanges and conversations, such as Leon Kahane, Anh-Linh Ngo, and Matthias Görlich to name a few.

Most of all, we would like to thank Stephan Trüby as our partner-in-crime in the larger research project, and for initially kicking off this project trajectory which is currently being developed into a special issue of *ARCH+* to be launched in the context of the forthcoming EU election in 2019.

For the artwork regarding the stone, we would like to thank photographer Enric Duch. For the design of the book, we are indebted to Pascal Prosek for initial research work, and to Sean Yendrys for the design and art direction of the book.

Thanks for all support from and at Studio Miessen, specifically Berta Cusó and Pablo Santacana, and everyone else there who helped us with this project. And last but not least, thank you to our families for their understanding and for bearing with us.

Material

Type	Times Ten
Paper	Munken Print White 90gsm Munken Lynx 240gsm
Printing	Four-color offset, with Brandlhuber+ Brown solid overprint on cover and symposium section

In August 2011, Berlin's major political parties were running their election campaigns. Though referring to very different ideologies, questions of urban policy became increasingly blurred—no real difference between stated policies on housing in Berlin could be detected. Following this lack of political differentiation, the architecture office Brandlhuber+ started a campaign pointing out this fact. By mixing the colors of the political parties—SPD (Social Democratic Party), Bündnis 90 / Die Grünen (Alliance 90 / The Greens), CDU (Christian Democratic Union), Die Linke (The Left) and FDP (Free Democratic Party) in equal parts, a brownish tone was created: RGB 165/96/36 CMYK 14/40/80/20. The question of and demand for a clear and strong color contrast raises the question of differentiation in politics. The color of political indifference was printed on monochrome posters and hung in public space, partly covering the existing election campaigns. It was shown on websites, in empty spaces, daily newspapers and public lectures. A public discussion began that initiated a debate over the ambiguities of the political color range.

Title	Para–Platforms
	On the Spatial Politics of Right-Wing Populism
Editors	Markus Miessen, Zoë Ritts
Contributors	Benjamin H. Bratton, Liam Gillick, Hannes Grassegger, Mahmoud Keshavarz, Angela Nagle, Nina Power, Patricia Reed, Konrad Renner, Slavs & Tatars, Jonas Staal, Hito Steyerl, Wolfgang Tillmans, Stephan Trüby, Christina Varvia (Forensic Architecture)
Design	Sean Yendrys
Printing	Printon in Tallinn, Estonia
Publisher	Sternberg Press
	Caroline Schneider
	Karl-Marx-Allee 78
	D-10243 Berlin
	www.sternberg-press.com

ISBN 978-3-95679-392-9

© 2018 the editors, the authors, Sternberg Press. All rights reserved, including reproduction in whole or in part in any form.